GW00835835

Mr Andoh's Pennine Diary

Koichi Andoh

Mr Andoh's Pennine Diary

translated by Takayoshi Andoh
and edited by Stephen Curry

Published by Royd House
The Book Case
29 Market Street
Hebden Bridge
West Yorks.
HX7 6EU
www.bookcase.co.uk

© Stephen Curry, 2011
diary@searchlight.plus.com

Cover photo & design: Stephen Curry

ISBN: 978-1-907197-06-2

Acknowledgements

I am grateful to Takayoshi Andoh for allowing me to work with him on his father's diary and for his helpful responses to my many questions about his family's past and other related questions about Japanese life and culture.

I would like to mention the late Lloyd Greenwood, who in 2001 took the time to show Takayoshi around the Fairfield area where his father had lived and worked as recorded in his diary. Lloyd also told me much about the folk who ran local hatchery businesses. He was able to put names and faces to many of the people in a 1935 photo album relating to the diary, some of which are included in this book.

Likewise I would like to thank Rod Watson for also identifying people on some of the photographs, and Mr Robert Parker for providing me with some invaluable documents about the chick sexing techniques taught locally during this period.

And my thanks also go to Professor Hirunagi of Nagoya University for providing me with a copy of a 1936 training film for Chicken Sexing, which brought to life the nature of the work recorded in this book.

All of the documentation produced by my research into the history of the local hatcheries has been deposited in the archives of the Hebden Bridge Local History Society, including a copy of the above training film.

My gratitude also goes to Jim Botten, who proofread for me during this process and made helpful comments about the text, layout and ultimately the comprehension of some sections.

And finally thanks to Felicity and Kate of Royd House Publishing for guiding me through the final stage to get the book printed and on the shelves.

Takayoshi Andoh with Lloyd Greenwood at
Angeldale Guest House in 2001

Contents

Illustrations

The main source of the photos in this book is the private photo album of the Andoh family.

Photos of the Greenwood grave and urn are by S. Curry.

Thanks to Mildred Butterworth for lending the Finney Bros. brochure.
The photograph of the 'blinking lights' on the Pack-horse Bridge to celebrate George V's Silver Jubilee was taken by H. Stansfield. An original copy can be seen in the Local History archive.
Thanks to Mr Derek Sutcliffe for use of any of the pictures via Mr Andoh which may have originated from his parents.

Introduction

The words 'Chicken Sexer', to the uninitiated, generally give rise to an inquisitive smile and often to a more entertained reaction. I have to admit that when I was first introduced to the topic, I too was somewhat amused at the job description. However, once over my initial reaction I came to understand that this line of work was a highly skilled and valued occupation for the profitable chicken hatchery businesses of the Calder Valley from the 1930s to 1960s. In fact it became a critical sub-contracting requirement for hatcheries all around the world. Even today expert 'sexers' are still widely employed.

It is generally acknowledged that Japan was the origin of the modern skill of determining the sex of chickens and there are references to 'Japanese visitors' in local history documents in the areas where hatcheries were a significant industry. The focus in this book is on the journey of one such Japanese chicken sexer, his work and the activities of Japanese colleagues, who came to the Calder Valley in the mid 1930s to work and train local hatchery workers in the art of 'sexing' one-day-old chicks. One would think that a job so repetitive by nature would be somewhat boring: however to the contrary, it appears that for this man the journey and the time spent here in a strange and foreign environment, were far more irksome and it was his pride in his work which kept him engaged and contented.

This is the story of Koichi Andoh, a man in his mid-twenties, who set off in November 1934 from his home port of Nagoya on board an NYK Line steamer called the *Hakusan Maru*. After six weeks at sea he reached London and eventually arrived in Hebden

Bridge by train in the New Year of 1935. He spent about five months in the town working for F & T Lumb's Hatchery and helping to train their workers in the sex distinguishing techniques. F & T Lumb also advertised his services in the *Hebden Bridge Times* to other poultry establishments.

HAVE your **CHICKS SEXED** by **JAPANESE** Expert. — F. and T. Lumb, Fairfield, Hebden Bridge.

Koichi kept a diary from the day he set sail to the day he returned home. The diary was not meant to be a literary work, it is a simple record of his long journey and time spent imparting an unusual skill to an alien culture. It provides a daily snapshot of his experiences and emotions whilst here and of working life in the valley's hatchery businesses. It is thus a unique insight into a specific period of the valley's history. The contents of the diary offer aspects of an adventurous journey made by a young man and the culture shocks he encountered along the way. It depicts his personal roller-coaster emotions of joyful highs coming from great job satisfaction, and the lows of social boredom, melancholy and his more than apparent homesickness. He also reveals something of his spiritual side without indicating any particular religious beliefs.

Nearly 70 years later in 2001, Koichi's son, Takayoshi, visited Hebden Bridge in a bid to trace his father's footsteps. He arrived clutching the original handwritten diary and about fifteen entries which he had already translated into English himself. Takayoshi's elderly mother Kimi had only told him of the existence of the diary along with a photograph album in the late

2

1990s and until then he seems to have known little about his father's life. It now feels almost fated that the Tourist Office should have placed 'Mr Andoh' with us at Angeldale Guest House. After we had got over our aforementioned jocular reaction to 'Japanese Chick Sexers' we thought the subject was sufficiently interesting to present Takayoshi to the local and regional press, who willingly covered his story. To this day in Japan he proudly carries the resulting *Yorkshire Post* article[1] with him! I personally became more and more fascinated by the diary and the idea of a young Japanese man boarding a steamer in 1934 and travelling halfway around the world to sex chickens. I also began to realise that the chicken breeding business was a piece of local history which had largely been forgotten, overshadowed by the cloth and clothing industry for which the town is better known. This led me to begin researching the local hatchery history for myself.

In terms of the diary, Takayoshi willingly set about translating the whole journal for me. It was a painstaking exercise for him, because of the difficulty with the script, which was written mostly in an older style Japanese *(Bungo)*. This has been superseded today by a more modern script *(Kōgo)*. It was made additionally difficult because I asked him to translate the diary one entry each day starting on the 12th November 2002, the exact same day sixty-eight years after his father had left for England. Because I had read the brief translations already available without a visual reference to the time of year, I wanted to put myself chronologically in the shoes of Koichi Andoh and to try to experience his sentiments for the seasonal climate and

---

[1] See Appendix p. 132.

3

natural environment. (The Japanese have always been sensitive and observant of their natural surroundings. Ian Buruma in *A Japanese Mirror*[2] observed that 'Letters and post cards always begin with a short description of the season'.) Koichi Andoh made few exceptions to this cultural trait in his diary entries. The daily translation process also provided a motivation for Takayoshi to complete the task within a set period.

Takayoshi's command of English, by his own admission, is somewhat limited, but with his working knowledge of the older script and the aid of a compact electronic dictionary he dutifully managed to translate and email to me the entries day by day for six months. At times consideration was given to obtaining the services of a professional translator. However, like many of us who make a sort of spiritual journey via our family history research, this was the sort of journey Takayoshi needed and wanted to make for himself.

Many of the entries were still difficult to understand in the translated form, but where possible I have resorted to commonsense interpretations of the essence. However, I have left most of the broken English translations as they were sent to me: those texts are easy enough to interpret without correction. A full and word-perfect translation would, I doubt, bring forth further clarifications of any real importance. And I think it would possibly detract from the original flavour of Koichi's own lack of command of English. He is repetitive at times in his subject matters: work, weather, letter writing and his frustration of being away from home. But, the disjointed, ungrammatical and sometimes funny translation hopefully serves to lighten the more

---

[2] Ian Buruma in *A Japanese Mirror* (Penguin Books).

4

mundane entries. My hope is the reader will enjoy the quirky style, as I did on receiving my daily drafts.

As well as setting the diary and Koichi's trip into a brief historical context, I have in places added some explanatory information about Japanese culture and the politics of the time to aid understanding of Koichi's own questions about, comments on, and sometimes discomfort at, the British way of life.

Working with Takayoshi to bring this diary to print has also been a personal journey, both through the background literature I needed to explore and my resulting trip to Japan in 2010, where I was the guest of Takayoshi, his three children, their spouses and his nine grandchildren. This experience has led me to examine the many stereotypical misconceptions I'd held about the Japanese, both in the past and the present.

I am of course extremely grateful to Takayoshi and his family for allowing me to present this unique diary to a wider audience. And for allowing me to use the entries as a basis for a future, more creative work.

All Takayoshi has asked of me is, that his father's published diary will be dedicated in some way to international peace and friendship.

The Historical Context

In the mid-1920s the chicken supply industry was pre-occupied with finding ways in which chickens could be sorted early in their growth into male and female. This sorting was required so that breeders could pass on the maximum guarantee to farmers that they would receive chicks which would develop into egg-laying hens. Until the 1920s most breeders used the methods of either breeding a particular type of chicken which, for example, had prominent sex differences in their wings at an early stage of growth, or else they waited for a 4-6 week growth period after which most breed's 'secondary sexual features' could be identified.[3] Neither of these methods were helpful in satisfying the efficiency demands and financial rewards of birds being shipped as soon as possible from breeders to farmers.

The main problem they identified was that the sexual organs of chickens were located internally and were not easily visible. Even internal examination didn't appear to show any distinct differences in chicks. The Japanese persevered in their studies and by the late 1920s they had developed a method called 'vent sexing'. This technique entails picking up a chick, gently squeezing it so that its vent excretes faeces, after which the internal organs become visible. The expertly trained eye can then distinguish the slight bump in the vent which (generally) indicates the bird to be male. In addition to this sexing technique it was important to develop the speed at which a sexer could make the distinction and thus how many chicks could be processed per hour. The Japanese also worked on

---

[3] Dr. Tommy Nakayama - *American Poultry History.*

6

productivity techniques and early claims stated that skilled operators could process between 30-50 birds a minute.

The world depression in the early 1930s brought in requests from US, Australian and European breeders for the Japanese to send sexers to work and train their local hatchery workers in a bid to help them become more productive and competitive and thus to stay economically viable. The Japanese had by then set up a school in Nagoya to teach and train sexers for this purpose. The industry standard for the most experienced sexers in the mid-30s was about 1000 chicks per hour at a 98% accuracy.[4] However despite having the advantages of this new technique, by 1935 it was clear that the depression was also hitting the previously fast developing chicken breeding industry world wide.

After World War II there were theories that the Japanese sexers had probably come here to spy or to learn about the British people in preparation for challenging the British Empire in the Far East. The theorists pointed to the fact the chicken sexers stopped coming to England around 1936-37. In his diary Koichi clearly becomes aware of crisis talks among local hatchery owners about the effects of the depression and he, for one, was not expecting to be invited back to work in the years that followed. So the disappearance of the Japanese sexers in the late '30s seems more likely to be due to economics than to preparation for war. There is no doubt that, throughout the 1930s, the Japanese military were devious in hiding their long-term plans and as they were on a war footing in Asia during this period it is likely they would have done their 'British

---

[4] Ibid.

research'. But it is doubtful that ordinary people like Koichi were a part of an elaborate intelligence-gathering exercise. In fact the general public in Japan were said to have been as surprised as the rest of the world was, when their navy attacked Pearl Harbour in December 1941. An Englishman, John Morris, living in Japan at that time wrote *'For the first few days there was an air of bewilderment about the people; nobody seemed quite to believe that Japan had actually entered the war.'*[5]

It is a fact of history that Japan in the 1930s was a nation asserting itself in Asia. It was late in becoming a modern industrial nation, only having moved on from a feudal government in 1868. The Japanese economy grew at a tremendous speed in the late 1800s and it became a dominant power in the region. Their early expansionist desires saw them firstly defeat the Russians in Manchuria in 1904-5, Korea was annexed by 1910 and in 1931 they again invaded Manchuria to remove the Chinese and take full control of that region. The League of Nations criticized Japan for their aggressive encroachments, but could do nothing to prevent them.

A simple analysis of that period is that the military gained popular nationalist support from the general population for its advances in Asia. In the tensions and conflict with China, the Japanese military imposed 'solutions' before political policies were established. This resulted in a general feeling of national pride which appeared to endorse the combative actions. Some elements of the military took a stance against the democratically elected politicians who were regarded as

---

[5] John Morris – *Traveller from Tokyo* (The Book Club 1942). John Morris lived and worked as a lecturer in Japan for the Japanese Foreign Ministry during between 1937–1941.

too westernised, weak and corrupt. And between 1934-1936 certain factions of the army plotted and carried out assassinations of government ministers.

In Britain in the mid-1930s the political atmosphere was one of alertness to the threat of international conflict. In 1935 the nation voted in the 'Peace Ballot' which was an attempt to gauge British feelings on membership of the League of Nations and world security matters. There had been a nervousness in 1933-34 about the militarism in Germany and their conscription project. There were also concerns about the tensions between Japan and China. According to Anthony Eden, 1935 was to be a year of slightly more 'cheerfulness'. As it turned out, 1935 saw Hitler establish the Luftwaffe and introduce the Nuremberg anti-Jewish Laws.

In Hebden Bridge, as in most of the country, a positive vote was recorded in the Peace Ballot, meaning support for the League of Nations, a reduction in arms production and support for collective world security. At the same time unemployment in the town was reported as 748 by the *Hebden Bridge Times*, around 300 of these being temporarily laid off. (Nationally unemployment was running at about 20%.) Also reported was the downturn in the trade of the velvet and cord manufacturers. Thus it was a time where economic and trade confidence was very low.

It was against this uneasy international political background and the difficult local and world economic situation that the ordinary people of Hebden Bridge and visitors like Koichi Andoh tried to continue normal life and commerce. They were uncertain times when Koichi set off on the 6000-mile journey from his home in central Japan. He came with several colleagues; some to Hebden

Bridge and others who went to places like Kent, the South Coast, the Midlands and the North. The names and locations of those mentioned in the diary, I have listed in Appendix 1 at the back of this book.

The Diary

November 12ᵗʰ 1934

2pm I left for London, England from Nagoya port with Mr Itoh and Mr Kuno.

I went to bed at 9 o'clock.

The SS Hakusan Maru

November 13ᵗʰ 1934

The ship docked in Osaka [*second biggest city in Western Japan*].

I got up at 6am and washed my face.

By 8am, I had had my breakfast.

I went sightseeing in Osaka.

At noon it was started to rain. I returned our ship and took lunch, and then relaxed in the smoking room.

3.30pm, our ship left Osaka Port for Kobe City Port.

About 5pm, in the rain, our ship entered port in Kobe.

After the diner, I went to see sightseeing in Kobe City, came back our ship at 11pm and went to bed.

November 14th 1934
In the morning I looked around Kobe City and paid a
visit to Minatogawa Shrine [*a shrine dedicated to the spirit
of Kusunoki Masashige, a famous chieftain during the
Nanbokucho period of 1336-1392*].
I took a bath in the city and came back and went to bed.
[*Communal bathing in bathtubs with very hot water was, and
is, a typical Japanese pastime.*]

November 15th 1934
8am, I got a telephone call on board from Mr Yamaguchi
[*the Chairman of board of directors of the Japanese Chicken
Sexing Association*].
8.40am, I went to Sannomiya Station to met Mr
Nishitani. [*See Appendix 1 on colleagues.*]
I took tea with Mr Ise, Mr Sugano, Mr Kumei, and Mr
Yamaguchi at Hotel Omori [*all members of the association*].
And later we had lunch together at Restaurant Kikuyu.
I came back to our ship and waited to leave at 3pm.
There was enormous numbers of people at the 'send-off'
at Kobe Port.
Our ship then set sail for the west to the Seto Inland Sea.

November 16th 1934
Our ship anchored at Centre of Kanmon Straight and I
look rounded in Moji City. I went to see the city sights. I
stayed there one night. This city was not so big.

November 17th 1934
9am, I came back our ship by a launch.
12.30pm, our ship left Moji Port for Shanghai.

November 18th 1934
During the daytime, our ship did not pitch and roll but
in the night I got seasick.
The muddy stream of the Yangtze River was very
terrible.

November 19th 1934
At about 9am, we arrived in Shanghai.
In the afternoon, I looked rounded in the city by car and
after dinner I took a walk, 8 peoples altogether. We
dropped into 'Café Lion'. I could see a lot of Jinrikisha's
[*Rickshaws*] in the town. I got back our ship at midnight
and went to bed.

November 20th 1934
The ship left Shanghai head straight for Hong Kong at
7am this morning.
It was clear and comfortable today.
Tonight was the fifteenth night of a lunar month, we
could see a beautiful full moon, the China seashore to
starboard. The ship ploughed the waves and went
straight for Hong Kong to the south. There was no
rolling and pitching. It was very calm night.
I went to bed at 9pm.

November 21st 1934
The ship continued straight for Hong Kong to the south.
I have got used to voyage, I felt good. I went to bed at
11pm.

November 22nd 1934
I got up at 7.30am and enjoyed myself on the deck all
through the day.

Tonight's the moon was very beautiful too. I became to be sentimental every time I saw the moon. About 10pm we arrived at Hong Kong and I went to bed.

The expected time of arrival was tomorrow morning but it will advance the time early a little, because of a following wind. It was a very beautiful view that all over the mountain were decorated by illuminations.

November 23rd 1934
In the morning, I landed in Hong Kong.
I climbed to the place which we commanded a view of Hong Kong Port by a cable car.
The view was more beautiful than Shanghai's one.
In the afternoon, I went ashore again and walked around the city.
The exchange value of Japanese money. It was very high rate.
Before dinner, I got back our ship.

November 24th 1934
At 11am, the ship left Hong Kong and headed straight for Singapore.
The wave was very quiet. It was a calm sea.

November 25th 1934
A calm sea, today.
After dinner, we practised a Japanese group dancing named 'Tokyo Ondo' on the deck. *[Ondo is a traditional Japanese folk festival music for song and dance.]*
I went to bed at 10.30pm.

November 26th 1934
Quiet voyage. It was pleasant.
From 8.30pm, I saw a movie in the first-class cabin.

It started rain and was very much hot.
I went to bed at 11.30pm.

November 27th 1934
It was very good weather this morning but very much hot.
It was completely like the middle of summer.

November 28th 1934
Our ship went forward Singapore on the mainly cloudy sea. At noon, it entered port.
The thing that I could see was green grasses the whole surface.
A native Malayan dived into the sea from the small boat and picked up nickel coins that the passengers threw for charity from the ship. The performance was splendid. I was surprised very much but I felt a little sorrowful.
Black as coal native peoples got on the ship.
It was rain from morning and became a light rain in the afternoon.
I bought 150 cigarettes for 1 yen 27sen, and 7 picture postcards for 50sen.
After teatime at 3pm, I went sightseeing in the city.
This city's transportation was rail-less street cars [*trolley buses*].
And I took a jinrikisha [*Rickshaw*]. I made visit to a museum and learned a great deal from there. After dinner at 6.30pm, I had a little rest.
I could see many tropical plants, for example palms, bananas etc.
Almost all these things were new to me.
In the evening I engaged in a long conversation with a ship's steward. His experiences were very interesting.

I went to bed at 11pm.

November 29th 1934
I stayed on the ship in the morning.
Some peoples came to our ship to sell all sort of goods.
I went to visit the Osaka Shosen* ship of emigration for
Brazil. [*A merchant ship company in Japan]
At noon, our ship left Singapore. In the afternoon, until
dinner, it was very hot.
I saw the sun set to starboard and our ship went toward
the Northwest.
After dinner, it became be very cool. The wind was high
and caused big waves but our ship did not pitch and roll
too much.
I went to bed at 9.30pm.

November 30th 1934
I got woken up at about 2.30am by the irregular sound of
a whistle.
It was heavy rain. The natives who got abroad from
Singapore were on the deck and acting confused. The
propeller stopped and the ship sounded the whistle
continuously and stopped.
In the morning, it was very fine weather and very hot.
Our ship entered port into Penang at 6.30pm.
After dinner I went out to sightseeing in the city.
Unfortunately it started to rain.
It was beautiful town. There were Gokurakuji [*Buddhist
paradise temple*], Hebidera [*snake*] temple and other
temples that we thought of old times.
I came back to the ship at 9.30pm.

December 1st 1934
It was a cloudy and cool day today.

I did not go shore because of I got tired terribly last night.

Our ship's sailing time was at midday but it was delayed until 5pm.

A jeweller came up to our ship and jewellery was very cheap.

At 5pm, our ship left Penang heading for Colombo.

December 2nd 1934
It was cool and a calm sea voyage.
I felt bored because I had no work to do.

December 3rd 1934
It was comfortable in this morning but I had no appetite and felt weary.
I had no fever. My bad physical condition was maybe caused by a shortage of exercise.
Afternoon, I played billiards on the deck.
Dinner was Japanese dishes and it was very delicious.
We watched the movies this evening.

December 4th 1934
All through the day, it made a voyage.
The ship was pitched and rolled considerably.

December 5th 1934
At midday, we arrived in Colombo.
I looked round in the city from 4.30pm.
Tonight at 11pm, our ship will leave Colombo for Aden.
We went to see the sights of the city streets.

December 6th 1934
It was fine weather but as might be expected of the Indian Ocean, a wave was very high.

Pitching and Rolling was strong. A wave went up to the deck.

I felt all right. The sea calmed down in the evening.

I talked many things with a next door Westerner in the evening.

I thought that it served practice for my English.

December 7th 1934

All through the day, it had quiet voyage but my feeling was not well. I spent time reading and then I spent some time chatting with my friend Mr Sugano in his cabin.

I went to bed at 11pm.

December 8th 1934

I felt good from this morning and enjoyed on the deck.

The sea was calm and I could see no land only water.

At 2pm our ship passed the *Fushimi Maru [a sister ship]*.

Its expected time of arrival in Japan is just before New Year's Day.

Our ship's the expected time of arrival in London is New Year's Day, too.

I was reminded of that our ship be returning to Japan in this sea area.

Both ships greeted each other. We could not see this spectacle expect when travelling at sea.

Both ships wished the other ship a safe voyage with hoisted a semaphore flag at the stern.

This evening, the movie was put on the screen. It was a interesting Sakura Ondo and Tokyo Ondo *[Japanese folk music and dance mentioned before]*.

I went to bed at 11pm.

December 9th 1934

We had fine weather and were on safe voyage today.

Our ship will intend to enter Aden Port in the morning on 12th.
I was really bored with the life on board.

December 10th 1934
I read books on the deck after breakfast. I could see considerable two big islands and had sight of a steamer to starboard.
We were told that our ship would enter Aden Port in the early morning on 12th.
I took an afternoon nap until at 3pm. And from 3.30pm, I joined the 'Deck Party'.
Boys [waiters] who wore female dress served us with ice cream, ice coffee, ice tea, Azuki bean soup with rice cake and agar-agar [jelly] cubes and other delicacies in sugar syrup etc.
It was very lively on our ship. I went up on the deck after dinner, there was very beautiful sunset.
I didn't know what day it was today by the old [lunar] calendar but I guessed probably a new moon tonight. I saw countless stars by the chimney at the left side of our ship.
The moon reminded my homesickness. I already spent life on board ship about one month.

December 11th 1934
A wave was calm and the ship didn't pitch and roll. I was comfortable.
I got a sleep for after lunch to four o'clock.
At night, I was felt for some time loneliness by seeing of the moon.

December 12ᵗʰ 1934

I waked up early morning because of I took a nap yesterday. So got up at five o'clock and took a walk on the deck. It was dark but I began to see faintly the light of Aden Port. At 6pm, our ship anchored there. After breakfast, I went to see the sights of Aden town. The town smelled nasty. The origin of bad smells was camel and goat's dung I think.

There were mountains but they were all rock mountains. There was nothing a tree in that place.

I could see only a herd of camels and goats. I heard that there was the real town behind the mountains.

The sailing time was at 11pm, therefore I came back to our ship by a launch at quarter to ten. This ship left Aden Port and entered the Red Sea, the hottest zone on the NYK's ship's regular European line.

December 13ᵗʰ 1934

After breakfast, I went up the deck and saw islands here and there but there are no trees.

Fifteen or sixteen albatrosses came flying and scavenged for feed. It was very hot that the Red Sea was. I took an afternoon nap after lunch to 2.30pm depended on an electric fan.

We crossed each other only two boats in the morning through whole today.

In the afternoon, we couldn't see even one island.

We could see merely extensive seawater.

Tonight we watched the movies.

December 14ᵗʰ 1934

This morning at about five o'clock, it was rain.

I had heard that it had not rain all the year round in the Red Sea but it was not true.

The ship went forward in the north west.

It was very cool and a wave was quiet.

I could not see other things except a boundless ocean, seawater.

From afternoon, it became an adverse and cool wind.

December 15th 1934

I got up at 6am and went out into the deck.

I welcomed the sunrise at 6.40am. I saw sunrise for the first time on this boarding.

The weather was good and comfortable.

Today, I felt a little cold rather. I don't feel heat even though in the Red Sea.

At just 9.30am, a steamship named the *Hakozaki Maru* *[another sister ship, higher class]* passed each other we saw her to starboard she was sounding a whistle.

From 6pm, we had Shukiyaki party *[sing song]* that was a successful meeting.

The passengers danced Tokyo-ondo, Western dance and so on. They were very lively.

December 16th 1934

It was fine weather and comfortable.

Although here was the Red Sea, I felt slightly cold in this morning so I changed from my summer suit into spring and autumn one.

From this morning I could see continue sight land on both sides.

I thought that Suez was drawing near. About 11, our steamship entered port of Suez.

I saw like the sand field where bare of trees. I thought this must be really a desert.

I could watch albatrosses they followed for our ship.

Around Aden, white birds were big and black ones were a little small.

The size of birds near here was about like pigeons and all colour was white. A wing got mixed a little black.

I could see the continued big mountain similarly a sand hill or a rocky mountain.

I heard that we could go ashore here and see the sights in Cairo, Egypt.

It took about 150 yen with Japanese currency.

A little before six o'clock our steamship left Suez Port and got into the Suez Canal at last.

Unfortunately, because of night I could not see scenery of both the banks.

But it was a moonlight night, I could see the sands of Arabia and saw a steamer to starboard.

On the left side, I could see lights here and there, it was probably the tip of the African Continent. The red and blue lights continued here and there on both ends of the ship's course.

December 17th 1934

It was sunrise at about 7am.

Our ship was late arrival in Port Said because of sea fog. Speed was 5 nautical mile an hour, it was slower than bicycle.

Our ship went forward north westward and right side landscape was a sandy plain of the Arabia Desert. In left side, Africa side, there were houses, trees and passage-ways parallel with canal.

I could see telephone wires too. And it turned into ponds, like marshland in the distance.

Our ship whistled a warning and went slowly in the sea fog.

About 9.30, our ship arrived in Port Said.

I exchanged money for 20 yen and we went ashore after lunch.

The fee of guide in the city was two pennies per one passenger.

I noticed in Port Said City that Egyptian women's style of dress was funny and interesting. They put the gold on top of nose, pulled black clothes over their head and whole body and had wore a mask but exposed only eyes.

I had seen the statue of the Frenchman, Ferdinand de Lesseps [developer of the Suez canal] on the south entrance and a bronze statue of two Australian Cavalrymen. The horses that they rode were beautifully made articles. [The 1st Light Horse Brigade protected the canal in WW1.]

The market in the city was very crowded but stank.

Today, I withdrew 40 yen from the office and balance of my money became 140 yen.

The ship discharged above 10 thousand tons cargo in this port. It was very noisy because of sound of the winch. I could not stand noise with rattling of the upper part of the dining room.

Tonight at 11pm our ship leaves for Naples, Italy.

December 18th 1934

Last night at 11.30pm our ship left Port Said but I didn't watch as I was sleeping because I got tired from sightseeing of the city. It was rain once in a while and our ship pitched and rolled considerably. I felt sick a little but it was not so much.

Before dinner I felt sick as the ship continued to pitch and roll. I put a pickled plum [traditional Japanese very hot pickle] on my navel. I felt that it worked instantly for my sickness.

After lunch till at tea time, I wrote letters to my relations and friends.

December 19th 1934
Because of the Mediterranean Sea, our ship pitched and rolled a lot since last night.
I took my seat for breakfast but I didn't feel that I could use my chopsticks.
I ate the first mouthful but I stopped to eat and I went on deck. I felt seasick and I went to bed in my cabin. I didn't take lunch or dinner.
After bathing, I ate three piece of vinegary rice rolled in seaweed [a kind of Sushi]. It was very much delicious.
Tonight, the movies were put on screen but I didn't go there. I still felt seasick so went to bed early.

December 20th 1934
Sea condition was calm in this morning.
It was forgotten yesterday's rolling.
It was cloudy today's weather but the surface of the sea was very calm and quiet like oil was poured.
I had filled up my stomach at the buffet. It was tasty.
In the afternoon, I felt very cold. After bathing, I had a little rest until dinner.
In this evening, we had farewell dinner and it was booming.
After dinner, I went up the deck and could see the light of the Strait of Messina.
I heard that we could see the Italian volcano Stromboli. I cancelled my nap today.
The wind blew strongly but our boat didn't roll.
We will arrive in Naples at about 10am tomorrow morning. From here and we can visit Pompeii, town of death.

Our ship entered the Strait of Messina at 9am.
The illumination of both banks and the moon in the sky
are very beautiful. They were beyond description.
Perhaps, this evening, it will be a full moon.
I recollected my home country and hoped my family
was happy.

December 21st 1934
I asked a cabin boy to wake me up at midnight. I got up
at one o'clock and went on deck. I saw on left side, a big
mountain that was like a turned down mortar.
I couldn't have a clear view of the volcano, Stromboli,
that was erupting actively, because it was covered with a
cloud and it was moonlight night.
That volcano was one of a remote and lonely island off
Italy.
I felt good this morning but our steamer pitched and
rolled much.
At 9am in this morning, I saw a volcano, Vesuvius that
vomit a great of smoke in Italy. The City, Pompeii died
by this Vesuvius's the eruption 2,000 years ago.
We had approached to Naples in Italy. It was very
beautiful an island in left side. There were houses. I
heard that they were all resort villas.
At 10am, we arrived in Neapolitan port. The customs
officer's uniform looked like Napoleon's military
uniform.
Our plan was to go ashore in the afternoon. The port's
scenery seemed be Western.
I went to Naples sightseeing with another five colleagues
and one Indian.
Our guide's name was Ariny. We watched the Pompeii
Dance. The dance show was unusual.
We came back the ship at 4.30pm.

A Neapolitan carriage cart had two wheels. Two or three horses pulled a coach. Sometimes, I saw a coach that had four wheels. A cart's wheels were very big.
They run and run with making sound of clap coach-man's long whip.

December 22ⁿᵈ 1934

Last night, I was treated to alcohol by a next door man.
At 9pm our ship sailed from Naples and this morning, the wave is calm on the sea.
We had Japanese dishes for breakfast in this morning. The taste was very delicious.
It was at 3pm and the tea-time had passed and it was unchanged to calm on the sea.
At 4.15pm, our steamer was heading in the direction of due north, Marseilles, France.
I could see the island of Corsica where Napoleon was born on the left side.
The evening sun was on ten feet above the island of Corsica. I felt that it became too short on the daytime.
Now, this steamer was going to north-westward. The moon had appeared on the sea. I couldn't work out what day today was in the old lunar calendar. Anyway, it was the round moon.

December 23ʳᵈ 1934

This morning at 7.25am I watched the rising sun on a mountainside far away to starboard.
The steamer was sailing to the north, the Port of Marseilles.
The climate was just like to Japan. It was cloudy and strong wind.
On the deck, I felt a little bit cold with my hands and face. It was rain in small drops.

At 8.30am, the steamer entered port.

In the morning, five of us went to see the city sights and walked about there.

I received the first letter from my younger brother in the morning.

Because of it was Sunday today, the street stalls of second hand stores and general stores had opened and queues formed. It was pretty crowded there.

I heard that there were many interesting places in the city.

At about 10am the sun shined through the clouds. Until then it was cloudy. It became very warm.

At noon, I came back to the ship.

After the lunch I wrote a reply to my brother.

I got tired in the morning so I didn't go out again.

My friends, Mr Itoh, Mr Sugano and Mr Kuno went ashore in the city this afternoon.

Mr Kumei didn't feel well.

The port was the biggest port in Europe that there was, our ship didn't use the winch with a rattling noise this time. The crane of fixture in port had done loading and unloading noiselessly.

I felt be comfortable because our ship was very quiet.

After dinner, I went to see the city sights with my four friends. I went to the cinema.

I visited a hotel and returned our ship at 11pm and went to bed.

Next morning, at 6.30, the steamer will leave for Gibraltar.

Most Japanese passengers left the ship in the Port of Marseilles and it was then crowded with foreign passengers.

December 24th 1934

I could sleep very well.

This morning, I heard the sailing gong half awake in my bed.

At 7.30am, I got up and washed my face and went up to the deck.

It was rain and the wave motion was big. The ship pitched and rolled considerably.

Japanese passengers got fewer so I felt to be lonely very much.

I dozed off in my bed at 11am until the lunch.

It was slightly cold outside and I slept again until the tea-time.

I went out, it was very greatly cold and the movement of the clouds was bad.

It was on Christmas Eve this evening. After dinner I went to the pictures at the first class saloon. I watched five reel pictures for example 'Tokyo Ondo', 'Cherry Blossoms Ondo' and 'The All Japan Tourist Information'. The first class passengers were nine and the second-class one was crowded. After the movies, I went up on the left side deck, I could see the 'Three-stars' in the left side distance. I felt that our ship went forward to the south. I could see the nice moon in the sky on the back direction. Every time when I saw the moon, I reminded my home country in my heart.

It is Christmas Day tomorrow.

December 25th 1934

After breakfast, I went on deck. It was very good morning and was calm on the sea.

The morning sun shined on the port side and I could see the continued land to starboard.

The moon remained lightly over the mountain.

Our steamer was advancing southward.

It was very nice Christmas Day, I think.

New Year's Day in my country was more important than Christmas Day.

I wrote and sent correspondences to my friends and the company.

I didn't take an afternoon nap today.

I heard that we would arrive in Gibraltar in early tomorrow morning.

I went to bed at 11.30pm.

December 26th 1934

This morning, at 8am the steamer arrived in Gibraltar Port.

It was cloudy but it would be good weather step by step.

I could see the grass-grown mountain to starboard and I felt good.

The port, Gibraltar was a quiet port.

Almost all passengers left the ship by the launch at 9am.

From at that time it became to be lonely on the ship.

The schedule starting time was 11.30am but the steamer left port at 12.30pm.

It was considerably a strong wind. The ship was pitching and rolling severely.

I felt anxious about Bay of Biscay.

Our colleague, Mr Itoh had bought an octopus in Gibraltar Port.

We took dinner in company with five colleagues in my cabin. Mr Shinohara treated us to some Sake *[Japanese rice-based alcoholic drink]*. We drank ¾ ltr with five peoples.

The octopus was pretty delicious.

The ship was shaking.

I went to bed at 10pm.

December 27th 1934

From morning, the ship was considerably pitching and rolling.

I made Mochi-Tuki today *[Japanese traditional rice cake for New Year]*. I started on the deck in the morning. I took my apron used for sexing chickens from my suitcase and I pounded steamed rice in a big bowl making the 'Mochi'.

The ship came and went out of sight because of the high waves.

I had lunch in my room.

I got used to the sea travel now so I didn't feel bad so much.

December 28th 1934

From last night, pitching and rolling got violent.

This morning, our steamer entered into Bay of Biscay. It seemed to be a storm. I took breakfast in the cabin. The thing on the desk fell on the floor but I was well.

I took lunch in my room, too.

In the afternoon, I arranged my baggage.

The strong wind was howling, at about noon an antenna of ship's radio was broken but we had heard nothing. It was a violent wind and we had a big wave and at about 2pm, a cargo steamer went along to starboard. Our ship looked as if it was going to sink but fortunately the wind was favourable, for that reason our ship was comparatively easy.

December 29th 1934

I wrote and sent the post cards that I arrived peacefully to all the following.

All neighbours, classmates in the region, all the relatives, Mr Sueo Osada *[probably, his best friend]*, Komaki Chicken

Hatchery, The Farm Inagaki [*his hatchery of work*],
Tokeien [*literal translation – the East Chickens Farm,
probably another hatchery*] and many others.
It was very calm in this evening.
We will arrive in a port in London at 3pm, tomorrow.
I went to bed at 9pm.

December 30th 1934
It was very quiet last night and I could sleep well.
This morning, the pilot came on board.
At last, London drew near.
Weather got worse and it became rainy weather from
afternoon.
I felt somewhat cold on the deck. Just 2pm, we were on
the Thames now.
The water colour was light blue, but a little yellow
colour was mixed.
I could see ships everywhere.
At length, I would arrive in London after one hour.
At 2.30pm, we landed in Gravesend at that time it
became to be a bit dull.
We got on a train that started at 4.30pm, after just one
hour we arrived at Fenchurch Street Station. And we
went by taxi to the Hotel Hinode-ya [*a Japanese Hotel
meaning Sunrise House*]. There was no vacant room in
that hotel. Our alternative was to stay at Yamato Hotel
[*Yamato means Japan*]. I had Japanese food at dinner and
its taste was delicious.
Five of us walked around in the city until at 11pm and
we drank coffee with two suspicious women. I went to
bed at midnight, but I couldn't sleep because the hotel's
room was quieter than the cabin! Just before dawn, I fell
asleep!

December 31st 1934

In the morning, I got up at about
8am and had a bath.
I went out and bought a hat.
Breakfast in this morning was
Western-style food.
Mr Ikuta [*working permanently for
the association in England*] came to
see us.

Bought a Hat!

It was decided that all five colleagues
would be separated at this place.
Only Mr Kumei left this evening [*for Lydd, in Kent*].
Another four members will start tomorrow.
It was New Year's Eve, I was treated to Soba [*Japanese
traditional buckwheat noodles*].
At 7pm, Mr Yamaguchi [*must have taken a flight from
Japan!*] came.
We went to see the sights of London City with him and I
was treated to beer from him in the city.
It was crowded terribly in the city.
I went to bed at 11pm.

January 1st 1935

I slept well after a long time last night, until nine o'clock
this morning.
I jumped out of bed and took a bath. And then made
preparations of departure.
It was on New Year's Day, therefore I ate Zoni at
breakfast [*rice cakes boiled with vegetables*].
Mr Kuno [*Bolton*] and Mr Sugano [*Weymouth*] started
from here to their own destination by train at 11.50.
Colleagues remaining were only Mr Itoh and I. Our
departure was decided on tomorrow.
After dinner I went out on the town with Mr Itoh.
I went back to the hotel and went to bed.

January 2nd 1935

I got up at 8am, took bath and breakfast.

I was waiting for Mr Ikuta but he hadn't come.

I bought a bottle of pomade. It was 2 yen and 10sen. I was surprised for the high price of like that small bottle.

In the evening, at 5pm, we all left Yamato Hotel and went to Kings Cross Station and we departed from there for York at 5.30pm. The train arrived at York at 9.30pm. A Mr Spink came to the station to meet us. I was separated from Mr Itoh [stayed in York] at about 11pm.

At about midnight, I went for a walk with Mr Ikuta in York City.

Because of midnight, I couldn't see much but it was pretty town.

We saw the sights of the old, long castle wall.

January 3rd 1935

We started from York at 0.40am for Hebden Bridge.

On the way, we transferred at Normanton, Leeds Station.

I arrived at Hebden Bridge Station 5am.

After that, I visited Mr Thomas Lumb's house and woke him up and we talked together in the drawing room until at 8am. I lay myself down on the sofa and fell into a doze.

At 8.30, Mr Ikuta went back. I was left alone from then. I took breakfast.

I went to look on the hatching room and the growing room. There were about 20 sets of The Smith system [incubators] and they were growing chickens by the Battery. I thought that they were very good.

I was taken to near my lodging with Mr Lumb by his car.

At once, I changed from my ordinary clothes into working one.

I went again to my place of work and started to distinguish the sex of chickens.[6]

Two English young men there could distinguish quite well.

In the afternoon, I counted output and made an entry of them.

By reason of that I took passage on board as many as fifty days, I was anxious about my technical skill. But I was not afraid and I had a good record of distinguishing.

I was annoyed by I couldn't speak good English.

Later I presented an Japanese 'umbrella doll' to Mr Lumb as a token of my souvenir.

And to my hosts [Mr & Mrs Douglas], I presented Zori [Japanese sandals] and Kawara-senbei [rice crackers].

I went back my lodging and I took bath but hot water was too tepid. [Remember, the Japanese like very hot bath water!] At once, I fled out from the bathroom!

I was very lonely in my room that was the first floor.

The meal wasn't to my taste so I had difficulty eating it.

My lodgings were on the top of hill and a place with beautiful scenery.

I felt relieved for a while, I had arrived at my destination!

I wrote the letter for my home and I went to bed at 10pm.

---

[6] It is noticeable that Koichi Andoh was already eager to get to work! Later he often shows his prowess for sexing chicks at speed and in high quantities and he is also self-critical when he does not reach his own high standards.

Koichi Andoh in front of F & H Sutcliffe's Hatchery

From here on Koichi added the weekday to his entries [it is as if he needed a new reference point after his long journey where one day drifted into another].

January 4th 1935 (Friday)
I got up at 7am and prepared for attendance at work.
It was dark yet.
At 8.30am, I went to work and distinguished about 2,000 chickens.
It became to be interesting my job.
At 5.30pm, I came back to my lodgings, took bread and a bath.
I replied to the letter of Tadaichi [*a younger brother*], Mr Suzuki and Mr Ikuta.
I was disappointed by the rice porridge that got mixed with sugar for lunch today.

Tomorrow, there will be no chickens and the day after tomorrow is Sunday.
I went to bed at 10pm.

January 5th 1935 (Saturday)
There are no chickens to distinguish today.
I slept till at about 9am and I read books.
In the afternoon, I was taught English by the Hatchery owner's wife, Mrs Lumb. *[Amy Lumb, nee Hirst]*.
I went to see an opera with Mr and Mrs Lumb at a theatre 8 miles away *[Halifax]* by car that Mr Lumb drove. It was fun. At 9pm we came back and I visited the battery growing system house under owner's guidance. In that place, the facilities were complete with hot air sending *[incubation]* system from U.S.A. After, I was treated tea and the owner took me my lodging in his car.
I washed my face and went to bed at past 10pm.

Thomas & Amy Lumb

January 6th 1935 (Sunday)
I got up at 9am and from 10am, I went to got eggs with
Mr Lumb to take to Mr Kemp. We went back hatchery at
noon.
From 2pm, I took a walk with the landlord of my
lodging.
We went back home at 4pm.
I wrote a letter to a my grandparents.
It was shining the sun once in a while but all most all it
was cloudy and some time it was rain. In the evening, it
was a little cold.
I would work tomorrow so went to bed.

January 7th 1935 (Monday)
At just past 8am, I went to work.
Last night, it was fairly cold and this morning, I saw
frost.
In the morning, I had sexed over 1,000 chickens.
In the afternoon, it was not busy. I helped with to clear
up of the birth.
And I had done a little to sex chickens too.
After dinner, from about at 6pm, I went to the police
station to register with Mr Lumb and Mr Douglas by car.
I felt that it was same town, Halifax where I went to see
the opera on last night.
At my lodgings we got warm by the stove four peoples
with the grandfather at a downstairs room. This evening,
my lodging's wife was very glad because it will be her
elder daughter's third birthday tomorrow. Under the sky
of a foreign country, I felt that to be deeply thankful of
parental love.
I went to bed at 10pm.

January 8th 1935 (Tuesday)
I got up at 8.20am and went out of doors after breakfast.
It was pretty cold and felt miserable for it was not clear
weather, unsettled one.
In the morning, I had sexed chickens more than 1,000.
In the afternoon, there was no chickens and I helped to
put eggs into the artificial incubator. Because I felt odd if
I had idle away my time.
One of employees called me a German! Would you
believe one of employee called me a German! Of all the
things to say! I had resented this.[7]
I went back my lodging at about 5pm and took a bath.
I wrote letters hurriedly to my colleagues Kuno, Itoh and
Sugano.
I am bitter than anything else that I can not understand
English language well.
But Mr and Mrs Lumb and my lodging's wife are very
helpful peoples.
I have begun to feel interested about my job in England.
I was bewildered that there was so many kind of
chickens.
The incubators are not a that big though. The chickens
are very large and good. I am surprised at the very
careful selection of chickens when the chickens are sent
out.

January 9th 1935 (Wednesday)
It was very dense fog this morning. I couldn't see
literally an inch ahead.

---

[7] We can surmise that in 1935 in a small Yorkshire rural town,
simple untravelled working folk might have thought anyone
who looked different must be Hun! It's likely they only asked
inquisitively but were misunderstood.

And it was pretty cold, at about noon, it was look winter, I saw besides a snowfall.

In the morning, chickens hatched but no sexing chickens was done. I filled eggs into the incubator. In the afternoon, I had sexed 300 chickens.

After dinner, I wrote to Mr Yamaguchi and Mr Suzuki. I went to bed at 10pm.

January 10th 1935 (Thursday)

It was a mild day today, recently there were not many like this warm day.

In the morning, I sexed chicken about 1,400.

In the afternoon, I had no work and I wrote my brother a letter.

At 5.30pm, I went to the owner's wife to say hello on my way home from work.

I saw a moon seven days old above at the back of hill.

I had felt loneliness and went to bed at 8pm.

January 11th 1935 (Friday)

My landlady awoke me at 8am. I slept well last night.

I immediately made arrangements to go to work.

It was a rainy day since morning and a chilly day.

In the morning, I sexed chicken about 1,400 chicks. In the afternoon, I had no work.

I received the first letter from my friend, Suzuki at noon.

I replied to the letter in the afternoon.

I came back my lodging at 6pm.

Tomorrow, we haven't chickens, it is a day off.

Even after dinner and teatime, it drizzled on and off in the outside.

January 12th 1935 (Saturday)
It was very cold and a windy last night. It looked like snow too.
This morning at 9am, lodging's wife got me up after preparing to brew tea for me.
As I thought, it was a snowfall this morning.
I had the first experience to see a morning snow scene in England.
In the hatching room I washed my two pair of socks, an apron, and a fundoshi [*Japanese traditional underwear for men. See p. 146 for Mr Andoh in a fundoshi!*]
I was given cigarettes from Mrs Lumb. It was second time present of cigarettes for me.
In the afternoon, I was reading a book in front of a fireplace.
It became dark at 4pm and I felt that it was very long time per a day for me, because I was alone in the room.
I received the first letter from my colleague group, from Kuno.
It is Sunday tomorrow, in the evening, about 7pm, I was invited to go to the movies[8] by Mr and Mrs Lumb.
Unfortunately, I could not understand the language so it was not so fun for me.
All the spectators were watching the movie with a laugh but I was lost.
I went to bed at 11pm.

January 13th 1935 (Sunday)
It was as usual cold last night.
I got up at 9am and made arrangements for attendance at work.

---

[8] If you are interested to see what the movies were, see the list in Appendix 2.

I went for eggs to Mr Kemp's house with Mr Lumb.
When I started, I slipped and fell to the ground at the
way out of my lodging for freezing over.
The piled snow that was kept in the shade didn't thaw
and after all froze.
It was very cold outside. We went back the hatchery at
11.40am.
I talked with Mrs Lumb. I sexed chickens RIR [Rhode
Island Reds] types chickens over 30 at about noon. I went
back my lodging and took lunch.
Last night, on my way to my lodging from the cinema, I
felt heavy in the stomach.
At once I took Hyakusou [Japanese traditional herbal
medicine].
I hadn't a bowel motion but I felt good today.
At night it began to rain. I couldn't sleep until about
11pm as I'd had an afternoon nap.

January 14th 1935 (Monday)
I got up at 8am.
Fallen snow had thawed for a rainfall. A wind was
warm.
From 8.30am, until noon, I filled eggs into the incubator.
In the morning, I rechecked the male's chickens of RIR
type at Mr Watson's hatchery.
As a result, I found seven female chickens.
I wrote reply to the first letter from Itoh of my group in
lunch break.
Birth of chickens was late, therefore I sexed chickens in
the afternoon.
I sexed chickens and inspected over 1,000. The result of
my inspection was excellent.
After working, at 3pm, I visited Mr Lumb's home. His
wife's younger sister had been there. I enjoyed company

with them for little while and I was given some barley sugar.

I heard that Mrs Lumb is 49 years old. Mr Lumb is one year younger than her.

At 6.30pm, I drank tea, took a bath and had a little rest.

I went to bed at 9pm.

January 15th 1935 (Tuesday)
I went to work at 8.30am.

Two more Japanese peoples, Hattori and Taniguchi came to Mr Watson's house with Mr Ikuta.

I saw them and they were well. We enjoyed ourselves in the morning.

I wrote a letter to Mr Kuno.

I sexed chickens 1,400.

It was relatively warm day today but it was short in daylight.

After I took a bath, I talked to the landlord and his wife in front of the fireplace until 9pm but I couldn't understand almost all.

They had callers who were husband and wife.

At once, I went to bed.

January 16th 1935 (Wednesday)
I went to work in the hatchery at 8am but no hatched chickens.

I helped to put eggs into the incubator.

And I wrote a letter my friend, Suzuki and in the afternoon, wrote to my brother, Shunji.

I went back my lodging at 5pm.

One of a group, Mr Nishitani, visited my lodgings.

He brought the landlord's shoes that had repaired.

January 17th 1935 (Thursday)
In the morning, I distinguished about 1,000.
I received a letter from Mr Itoh and replied to him.
I wrote a post card to Inagaki Farm [his place of work in Japan] in the afternoon.
Today's my total distinguished chickens were more than 1,500 according to my recording.
The official number of the hatchery was less 100 than my recording.
But it couldn't correct the number because of I couldn't speak English.
At night, I wrote letters to Mr Kamio, Mr Ochiai and Mr Kennosuke Ishima who lives in London.
I felt to get warmer for the last few days.
I went to bed at 10pm.

January 18th 1935 (Friday)
My landlady woke me up at 8am, I jumped out of bed and went to work.
In the morning, I sexed chickens over 1,000.
I received a post card from one of a group, Kuno.
In the afternoon, I had nothing to do and I went to inspect to the hen house for a breed.
We loaded food onto our truck at the station and carried one to the hen house for a breed.
Our truck went forward at slow speed with buzzing 'Woo Woo' up the west the top of the hill.
Mr Lumb managed the hen house for a breed.
The view from the top of hill was very good.
The kind of hen for breed was 'Lord' type and 'Wyandotte' type.
There were pigs, dogs, horses and 6 or 7 cows in that grassland.
It was very nice scene that they were feeding on grass.

After got back, I sexed a few chickens.

At 5pm, I went back my lodging for tea, then took a bath.

At about 8pm, Mr Lumb came to take me to the hatchery and I sexed chickens 100.

Tonight, with Mr and Mrs Lumb went all together to the dance hall.

January 19th 1935 (Saturday)
I got up at 9am and had breakfast.

I went to Mr Lumb's house.

In the morning, I waited for coming letter in the hatching room.

From at 1.30pm, I went for eggs for breed to Mr Kemp's home.

I heard that Mr Kemp is a barrister.

It was a foggy day all day and it was nasty weather.

I wrote Tadaichi a letter [one of his brothers].

I went back my lodging but the landlady was out.

I wrote Saburo Kojima a letter [Sister's Brother-in-law].

I went to bed at 9pm

January 20th 1935 (Sunday)
I got up at about 8.30am.

After breakfast, I went to Mr Lumb's house at about 9am.

And I brought eggs to the hatchery of Mr Gregory that was 27 miles away from here with Mr Lumb. We went back from here at 12.40pm.

After lunch, I had a little rest.

My landlady said one of my group, Itoh comes here on 24th of this month.

I visited Mr Lumb.

I read a book and I went to bed in my loneliness at
8.30pm.

January 21ˢᵗ 1935 (Monday)
In the morning, there was no chicken.
Afternoon, I did my job, over 1,000.
I received the first letter from my father in the afternoon
and I replied it at night.
I wrote a letter to Yasuichi too [a cousin].
I felt that nowadays, it was a little warm.
I went to bed at 10pm.

January 22ⁿᵈ 1935 (Tuesday)
It was a dense foggy morning and cold.
I sexed chickens above 1,000 chickens in the morning.
Afternoon, it was not busy.
I was waiting for a letter from my home country
everyday but no tidings for a long time.
Pessimism!
I regretted that there was not enough work only a half
day every day.
Today, I did over 1,800.
After tea, I went to Mr Lumb's house and learned
English from Mrs Lumb.
It was very hard and I had difficulty.
I came back at 8.30pm. I talked with Mr and Mrs
Douglas by the side of the fireplace.
I could not understand them very well.

January 23ʳᵈ 1935 (Wednesday)
At 8.30am, I went to work but there was no birth of
chicken.
I washed my socks in the incubator room.

In the afternoon, I wrote letters to my brother, Tadaichi, Mr Niwa *[his town elder]*, Mr Matsunaga *[the head of the agricultural association]* and two relatives, Mr Yamaishi Inagaki, Mr Saburo Kojima.

It was a west strong wind and nasty weather.

After dinner, I wrote again letters to Toke-en *[East Chickens Farm]* and Komaki Kakin *[Komaki area Domestic Fowl Assoc.]*

Mr Thornber said to me that tomorrow morning, Moribe and Mr Ikuta come to the hatchery.

I went to bed at 10pm.

January 24th 1935 (Thursday)

From in the morning, it was rainfall.

I couldn't do job so much because of Moribe visited me *[Japanese colleague]*.

After lunch, I saw him to Mr Thornber's house.

It was nasty weather, wasn't it?

I sexed chickens 1,000 per a day, today.

At about 4.30pm, Itoh and Terazawa came to see me.

Terazawa returned with Mr Spink *[Mr Spink had a hatchery in Easingwold, York]*.

I went back my lodging with Itoh.

Moribe, Itoh and I talked variously till about 9.30pm.

I took a bath at 10pm and today's hot water of bath was very nice, comfortable.

And I went to bed.

January 25th 1935 (Friday)

From in the morning, it looks like a snowy sky. It was bad weather and very much cold, intense cold. From afternoon, it started to be a snowfall in earnest.

I had done over 2,000 today.

After dinner, I visited to Moribe's lodging at Mr
Watson's.

Mr Itoh played the piano. We enjoyed ourselves until
about 10pm and were treated to tea.

I went to bed at 11pm.

January 26th 1935 (Saturday)
I got up at 9.30am, It was the first fine weather today
since I came here.

In the morning, I went to confirm to the hatchery that
the letter for me had arrived but unfortunately it hadn't.

Afternoon, I went to attend the funeral of Hattori's
employer [Mr Dickie of Cowling] by Mr Watson's car
together three peoples. We came back at 4.20pm, I could
see quite unusually the sun but it was a strong wind and
very much cold.

I went to the cinema with the young man Marshall and
other one person and it started at 5.15pm and was over
at 8.30pm.

I played cards and enjoyed at Mr Lumb's house until
11.30pm.

I went to bed at midnight.

January 27th 1935 (Sunday)
Last night, I was out too much so I slept until at 10am.

Afternoon, with three colleagues, we visited to enjoy Mr
Watson's house.

From 6pm, I went to the hatchery and sexed chickens
200.

It was a snowfall today and intense cold.

I had a touch of cold so I went to bed 8.30pm.

January 28th 1935 (Monday)
I got up at 8am.

It was pure white on the whole surface in the out side.
In the morning, I had done above 1,000 chickens.
Afternoon, I was not engaged.
From today, the staff in the Hatchery office increased to two people.
Until evening, I had done 1,800.
I received the first letter from Taniguchi today and replied.
And I wrote the letter to Mr Okawa's family in near my home.
After dinner, at 7pm, I went to a barber's shop with my landlord and Itoh.
On our way back, we played billiards. The billiard table was different from Japanese one.
I went back at 8pm, took a bath and had a little rest. I went to bed at 10pm.

January 29th 1935 (Tuesday)
I got up at 8am and went to work but there was no new born chickens.
I did only the driver's assistant of truck for something to do with my time.
My lodging face north and there is a small hill behind it.[9]
Therefore, we can't see the sun for the sun passes the south direction.
From about 4pm, I did to sex chickens a little.
Itoh visited at the hatchery to use his idle time.
I went back with him.
I wrote Inagaki Farm a letter.
I went to bed at 10pm.

---

[9] *Evidence suggests this to be Palace House Road.*

January 30th 1935 (Wednesday)
Today, there was no hatched baby chicken.
I went to work at 8.30am.
I received a letter from Kumei and answered a letter.
I was idle at the office and it was severe cold out of doors.
Afternoon, I did above 200.
Itoh called on me.
From 2pm to 5pm, I took a nap at my lodging.
This evening, Moribe visited me.

January 31st 1935 (Thursday)
This morning, I got up at 7.30am and went to work at 8.30am.
I had done 2,800 chickens.
I didn't receive a letter from my home country so I felt lonely very much.
My taking a bath was after tea and after Itoh visited this Evening.
As usual, it was nasty weather and a cloudy sky, bad weather all day today, too.
I went to bed at about 9pm.

February 1st 1935 (Friday)
From morning, it was a rainfall.
It was not so busy today and I had done over 1,300 per day.
I received the first letter from Mr Kiichi Kojima [Brother in law].
At night, after tea I wrote reply to the letter for him.
I was presented a pencil by an office worker.
It is a holiday tomorrow and tomorrow afternoon, I intend to do that I will visit Mr Spink with my employer.

February 2nd 1935 (Saturday)
It was a day off from morning today.
I slept until at about 9.30am.
I went to the hatchery and washed my underclothes.
In the afternoon, I visited Mr Kemp with Mr Lumb and
another one.
It was sunny and good weather in the morning but
afternoon, it was a rainy and depressing weather.
This evening, Itoh and Moribe went to the cinema but I
didn't go to it because of a little cold.
They got back at about 9pm with getting wet with rain.
I talked of one thing and another with Moribe until at
11.30pm and went to bed.

February 3rd 1935 (Sunday)
It was strange weather from morning and started to rain.
The landlady brought breakfast to my room for me at
about 10am.
I was in bed until at 11.30am, then I got up.
It was a rainfall afternoon, I couldn't take a walk and
stayed at indoors.
I went to bed at 10pm after took a bath.

February 4th 1935 (Monday)
Unusually, it was a warm however, cloudy.
I went to work at 8.30am.
I received a letter from Terazawa and replied to it soon.
In the morning, I had done above 700.
Afternoon, I wrote my brother, Shunji a letter.
I hadn't a bath this evening and went to bed at 9pm.

February 5th 1935 (Tuesday)
It was warm morning and I went to work at 8.30am.
I received letters from Tadaichi [Brother], Chiyoko
[Sister], Mr Ishioka and Mr Kuno.
In the afternoon, I had no work.
At about 4pm, I picked up my pen to reply.
Itoh comes for me, and we visited Mr Spink with Mr
Watson.
I came back my lodging with Terazawa at 12.30am.
On my way back, it was a snowfall.
We used a car, it was better than on foot but I couldn't
stand that it took 2 hours on one way.
I went to bed but couldn't sleep and uncomfortable.
From 4am, I could sleep a little.

February 6th 1935 (Wednesday)
At 9.30am, I got up and took breakfast alone earlier than
others.
It was good weather in quite a while today.
In the morning, I visited Mr Lumb and Mr Watson's
house.
In the afternoon, Terazawa and I went to Hebden Bridge
Police Station with Mr Watson.
At 3.30pm, I returned and wrote letters to Tadaichi
[Brother], Chiyoko [Sister] and Mr Nakane [a neighbour].
And I replied to Mr Kuno.
It was cold outside.
At 9.30pm, I took a bath and, went to bed at 10pm.

February 7th 1935 (Thursday)
I got up at a moment before 8.20am and went to work at
8.30am.
Terazawa had come at about 9am.

In the morning, I was a little bit busy but free in the afternoon.

And so I went to the station by the truck to send out the chickens.

On the way to the station, I took chickens to Mr Watson's house.

From about 3pm, Terazawa had sexed chickens at Watson's house.

Today my finished chicken's number was 1,600.

I went back to my lodging at 4.30pm.

Every day it was depressing weather and I became tired of with this weather.

After tea, I visited Moribe and talked with him for about one hour.

I took a bath at 9.30pm and went to bed.

February 8th 1935 (Friday)
It was cloudy but from morning, very quiet weather.

Little by little, I had done sexing chickens more than 2,000 this day.

At 6pm, I had tea and took a little rest.

After that, I went to enjoy ourselves with Moribe and Terazawa to the town of Hebden Bridge.

On my way back, I stopped at Mr Lumb's hatchery and checked eggs for night work.

It is a day off tomorrow so until 11pm. Moribe and I had a chat with my lodging's husband and wife.

February 9th 1935 (Saturday)
It was a holiday in the whole day today

I got up at 10.30am and after breakfast I washed my socks at the hatchery.

I spend my time at Mr Lumb's home.

I got back my lodging at 1pm and next, I visited
Moribe's lodging next door.
I enjoyed a little and returned.
Mr Lumb went to Manchester by the truck from
afternoon. He went back the hatchery at 4pm.
It was unusually good weather today so in the afternoon,
I took a walk with Moribe to Thornber's hatchery. We
took a train on our return.
I visited Mr Kemp with Mr Lumb and Moribe by Mr
Lumb's car.
At 5.30pm, we got back and after tea, we had a chat and
I took a bath at 8pm and we had a chat again.
At 11pm, I went to bed and did reading.

February 10th 1935 (Sunday)
I got up at 9am and took a breakfast.
I read a book at downstairs room and took a nap from
1.40pm to 5.30pm.
After tea, I read a book again.
I was very bored on Sunday.
I will go to bed early tonight, too.
I went to bed at 8.30pm but I couldn't get to sleep
because of the afternoon nap.
I was annoyed by sleeplessness.

February 11th 1935 (Monday)
I got up at 8am.
It was not busy today, I had done over 700 in the
morning and afternoon, no work.
I dropped in at the hatchery.
After tea, I took a bath and went to bed.
There was no letter from my home country.
I was waiting for a letter from my country but I had
heard nothing. I became fed up with it.

February 12th 1935 (Tuesday)
I got up at 7.50am and went to work at 8.30am.
In the morning, I had done over 800 chickens and
afternoon, had rested.
I spent time at the hatchery.
After tea, I went into Hebden Bridge with Moribe and
Terazawa.
On the Tuesday, from afternoon to night, all shop closed
so it was very quiet. *[Half day closing.]*
But only the cinema was crowded and I watched a
movie once time.
I got back and had a chat with Moribe and Terazawa.
Probably, it was January 9, with the old calendar this
evening. *[Old calendar used in Japan and China based on the
reign of their respective emperors.]*
I could see the beautiful moon and I was getting
sentimental every time I saw the moon.
It is a day off tomorrow, Wednesday.
I went to bed at 10pm.

February 13th 1935 (Wednesday)
There was no chicken today and holiday.
Terazawa was woken up by the landlady at 8am and
went to Mr Thornber's house with Moribe. I was in bed
at 10am and the landlady brought breakfast for me at the
upper storey.
After wash my face, I took breakfast on the bed.
At 10.30am, I went to Mr Lumb's office to inquire arrival
of letters from home country.
Unfortunately, there was no letter and I got back in vain.
After lunch, I went to town with Terazawa and bought

one Karapin.*
Afternoon, I read a book but I was boring very much.
I went to bed after took a bath at 8pm.

Occasionally Koichi wrote words in Roman script, just as he had heard the word spoken. So if I tell you that we worked out that 'Ki Sori' was actually 'Keighley', 'Sonbus' was 'Thornber's, 'Arboreta' was 'Albert' ('Royal Albert Dock') and 'Sabati' was 'Summertime', you will see why sometimes normal interpretation or translation approaches are not enough. If you can work out what a 'Karapin' is, good luck!

February 14th 1935 (Thursday), (January 11th at the old calendar)[10]

Last night, it was a windy night but this morning was very quiet.
I could see the sun on my way to work.
Afternoon, it was rain. It was crazy weather truly!
I had done about 1,600 until 3pm.
I got back my lodging at 5.30pm and after tea, I replied to Itoh a letter.
Terazawa and Moribe went to a barber's this evening.
It was westerly windy night and nasty weather but the moon was good.
Sometimes I felt the moon was fine but sometimes a bad fellow.
I was getting sentimental and emotional.
I went to bed at 10pm.

---

[10] Koichi now has begun to record the Japanese calendar date equivalent at the top of his entries. This seems to be allied to his current emotions and feelings about his homeland.
However, he was guessing the corresponding date and therefore there seemed little to be gained historically by adding it here to each entry.

Left: Alan Marshall (F & H Sutcliffe's in background)

Japanese chick sexers with local ladies.

February 15th 1935 (Friday)
Last night, it was a windy night, too.
At 10pm, Terazawa returned from the cinema.
After that, I couldn't fall asleep until midnight.
This morning, It was rainy again.
It was busy in the morning and I sexed chickens over
2,000 per today.
Today, I received a letter from Shunji [*Youngest brother*]
and the 'Japanese Chicken Sexing Bulletin'.
I got back my lodging in the rain at 6pm and after tea I
answered letters and wrote a letter of sympathy for my
uncle of Kurumaya [*a relative and nearest neighbour*].
I went to bed at 10.30pm.

February 16th 1935 (Saturday)
I slept till about 10am and took breakfast on the bed.
And I went to the office to check coming to hand but no
letter.
This morning, Mr Lumb was out for the meeting of the
hatchery at Mr Thornber's house.
I washed.
Itoh came to see me with Mr Spink.
We took lunch with three colleagues and Itoh went back
at about 1pm.
I took a nap from about 2.30pm to tea time.
After tea, I chatted with Terazawa.
It was rainy weather all day today and a strong wind
from evening.
I went to bed at 11pm.

February 17th 1935 (Sunday)
At 9am, I got up and took breakfast.

I visited Moribe's lodging, Moribe took breakfast on his bed and Terazawa kept sleep so he didn't have breakfast.
I visited Mr Lumb's house and from 3pm, I went to buy cigarettes.
3.50pm, I returned and took a little rest.
It was cloudiness today but wasn't a rainfall.
After took a bath, I went to bed early.

February 18th 1935 (Monday)
In the morning, I had done over 1,000.
I went to the hatchery to be idle and received letters from Tadaichi *[brother]*, Inagaki *[Employer in Japan]*, Mr Suzuki and the association.
The letter said my uncle of Kurumaya died.
After tea, I wrote answer letters to four addresses.
I went to bed at 11pm.

February 19th 1935 (Tuesday)
In the morning, I had sexed chickens over 700.
Afternoon, I had no work.
After lunch, I wrote the answer's letter to Tyukinnsya *[a Japanese hatchery]* at the office.
I read books and had tea.
My watch glass was broken because I dropped it in the bathroom when I took a bath.
I will go to bed early to night.

February 20th 1935 (Wednesday)
I got up at 8am. I went to town to buy my watch glass at 9.30am.
On the way, I called at the hatchery's office to check the arrival letter.

But there was no letter. I visited Mr Lumb's house and spend my time there.

Afternoon, I wrote Mr Nishitani a letter and I took the letter to the hatchery's office.

It was a rainfall.

After tea, I took a bath at 8pm and went to bed at once.

February 21st 1935 (Thursday)
This morning, I got up at 7.40am.

Last night, I went to bed early. Therefore I woke up from sleeping at 2am.

After while, I couldn't fall asleep again and had a hard time.

It was very good morning today.

I had done 1,700 to 1,800 per day but I was half free in the afternoon.

In the evening, the hatchery was very busy with to send out chickens.

The employer, Mr Lumb was very busy, too therefore he didn't give easily me the signature.

At 6pm, I came back my lodging and tea.

There were no letter from anywhere. I was empty and I will go to bed early.

February 22nd 1935 (Friday)
At 7.30am, I got up and I had done about 1,700 chickens per day.

Afternoon, Moribe and Terazawa came to see me.

I got back to my lodging at 5.30pm.

I had tea, took a bath and went to bed early.

February 23rd 1935 (Saturday)
It was Saturday today.

Until at 9am, I was in the bed and took breakfast there.

I looked out of the window and it was a snowfall.

It was very cold indeed last night.

It was particularly good weather today and the brilliant rays of the sun.

In the morning, I washed at the hatchery.

I returned my lodging and wrote my English friend which was in English.

After lunch, I visited Mr Lumb's house and from 2.30pm, I went for eggs to Mr Kemp's house with Terazawa, Moribe and other one, four peoples.

It was crowded in Halifax on Saturday afternoon.

I got back, but it was too early for tea so we made a tour of Hebden Bridge town.

After tea, Terazawa and Moribe went to the cinema but I didn't go and read 'Yomimono' [*Translated was 'All Reading' - a Japanese light magazine*].

It seemed very cold outside.

At 9pm, after supper, I went to bed. It was good day today.

February 24th 1935 (Sunday)

It was good weather today, too.

But I felt that it was turned quite cold, for the last few days.

I got up at 9am and after breakfast I read books till noon.

From 2pm, I went to post office with Terazawa to posted letters addressed to Mr Ikeda [*a relative*] in Nagoya and my English friend.

Everywhere leaf buds began to appear so I felt that spring has come shortly.

I made a circuit of the town but the town in Sunday was deserted always.

A woman servant *[housekeeper?]* of Mr Lumb's was talking pleasantly with her boy friend in the town. I was envious of them.

After I took a bath, it started rainfall and I went to bed early.

February 25th 1935 (Monday)
I got up at 7.30am.
It was cold last night. This morning, it was a little snowfall.
At 8.20am I went to work and sexed chickens over 400. There was hardly any job in this morning.
After lunch, I went to see Moribe with Terazawa by train.
I helped a little him work.
We went back by train at 5pm and stopped at the office and got received two letters from Shunji *[youngest brother]* and Mr Nakane *[a neighbour]*.
After tea, at 6.30pm, we went out for a walk to the town. I posted two letters, had a haircut and bought a big-bowled bent pipe and Tobacco.
I smoked at the pipe but it was bad-tasting. I went back my lodging at 8pm.
It was very cold out of doors and I felt that it grew cold more from few days ago.
After supper, I went to bed.

February 26th 1935 (Tuesday)
I got up 7.30am.
It was cold morning but fine weather. It was unusual weather considering these days.
In the morning, I had done above 700 but afternoon, there is no chickens.
I visited Mr Watson's house.

From afternoon, it became a little warm, I felt. But ice in the shade didn't thaw.

It was very good day.

On my way home from Mr Watson's house, I stopped at Mr Lumb's house to check arrived a letter.

Unfortunately, there is no letter today.

At 4.30pm, I went back my lodging and took a short rest.

At 8pm, took a bath and after supper went to bed.

Terazawa and Moribe, went to the cinema this evening.

February 27th 1935 (Wednesday)

It was a day off today.

I felt very chilly even in my bed from last night to this morning.

I got up at 9am and as I thought, it was a snowfall.

It was dark and cold weather today.

After lunch, I took a nap from 2pm to tea.

It had stopped snowfall but it was very much cold.

I went to bed early, tonight.

February 28th 1935 (Thursday)

The landlady woke me up at 8am. I got up hurry and made preparations for going work.

At 8.30am, I went to work.

Last night, it was frozen over and very cold.

It was very busy today. I had done above 2,400.

It seemed that it was rain outside afternoon. I got back the lodging at 6pm.

After tea, I took a bit rest. I am going to sleep early.

Toward evening, it was very busy so I felt anxious about a result of sexed chickens in the latter half.

Today, I had done 300 chickens of the 'Lord' kind that belonged to Mr Gregory's hatchery.

I got receive replies from Kuno and Hattori.

March 1st 1935 (Friday)
I got up at 7.30am and went to work at 8.30am.
I had done over 1,500 per day. But afternoon, it was not busy.
In the evening, I helped with sending out chickens and arranging new hatched chicks.
I went back the lodging and after tea, took a little rest.
I received letters from Higashitanaka and Komatsuji [uncles] and Kumiko [cousin].
I got a reply from Kumei.
After tea, I wrote answer letters to Higashitanaka and Komatsuji
It is Saturday and a day off tomorrow, I will write the remaining answer letters then.
I felt it was a little bit warmer.

March 2nd 1935 (Saturday)
At about 9am, the landlady brought breakfast to my bed.
At 10am, I got up and went to Mr Lumb's hatchery to wash.
I sexed chickens 87 chickens in the morning.
On the way to the hatchery, I gave an order to a office worker to post.
I went to Mr Kemp's house with Terazawa at 2pm.
I went back my lodging at 4pm and took a little rest.
Moribe came to see me.
After took a bath, I went to bed.

March 3rd 1935 (Sunday)
It was Rain, cloudiness and fog.
It was Sunday today so I took breakfast on the bed, after I slept again.
At 12 noon, I got up and at 1pm took lunch and a little rest.

It was expressed very realistically famous country of fog by today's weather.

At 2pm, Moribe came to see me and I switched a light on because it was very dark in my room. I was bored very much on every Saturday and Sunday.

This evening, at 6.30pm, I went to bed very early after took a bath and tea.

The trouble was that I woke up at about 11pm so I read book for a little while.

March 4th 1935 (Monday)

7.30am, I got up.

In the morning, I had done about 500 chickens and afternoon, no job.

It was unusually good weather today and seems the weather was spring.

I could see the sun through the whole day.

It was very comfortable that bathing in the sun.

From 2pm, I went to the town to buy cigarettes.

It was an eye-popping price, very expensive, one shilling one piece [a packet? Or he bought a cigar!?].

I received a letter from my mother and wrote the reply at night.

After bathing, I went to bed.

March 5th 1935 (Tuesday)

I went to work in the rain.

In the morning, I had done over 500 chickens.

After lunch, there was no job.

It was very good weather this afternoon.

I replied to Takabatake's reply and posted letters to my mother and a relative.

I went to office to check the arrival letter but nothing.

I carried chickens to the station by lorry and went to see somewhere.

It is a day off tomorrow, I talked together in the next room till 10pm.
I went to bed at 11pm.

March 6th 1935 (Wednesday)
I got up at 8.30am, after breakfast I took a little rest.
I felt it was a rainfall last night. This morning, it was cloudy weather but white clouds were drifting in the sky and I could see blue sky here and there.
After lunch, I visited Thornber's hatchery with Terazawa.
In that place, I met a woman trainee for sexing chickens. She was 18 years old and very cute especially her mouth and her eyes.
She is too beautiful and cute for words. Her name was Miss West.
But her ability was not high and out of the question so I checked, again her judgement. As a result, she had made many mistakes! *[Truly an example of how Japanese work ethic is paramount. Even a beautiful girl cannot distract Koichi from his professional duty! And this brief encounter did spark further thoughts about the demonstrative British youth.]*

It was quite unbearable to me that the attitude of British young men toward women.
They did kiss and moreover, flirted with each other. I was vexed with them.

Alan Marshall and Esther Leah.

*[In 'Traveller from Tokyo', based in the 1930s, John Morris,
the author, states that marriage in 1930s Japan was 'less of a
personal thing and more of a family affair than it was in the
west'. Arranged marriages were still the usual way of couples
getting together. Therefore few couples would ever meet fall in
love and decide on their own to get married. He also observed
that Japanese did not connect love and marriage as we did then
and still do. Marriage for the Japanese was more about
procreation and preservation of family status. Suffice to say
that a boy and girl holding hands or cuddling in public would
be a culture shock of the highest order for Koichi.]*

At 5.30pm, I got back with other two fellows from
Thornber's hatchery and tea and a little rest.
Incidentally, I stopped at the hatchery to check the
arrival letter. But no letter.
I felt that in this circumstance of my job I was not able to
work to my maximum worth.
I had feeling that I had gotten a true lazy fellow in like
this job's condition.
But I will be able to do over 2,000 chickens.
This evening, Moribe came to see me.
Today's taking a bath was my turn. I would like to go to
bed early to kill time.

March 7th 1935 (Thursday)
At 7.30, I got up. It was warm and good weather today.
In the morning, a little bit busy.
At noon, I received four letters from Japan and two of
them were from my brothers.
After lunch, I wrote replies to Japan at the office.
Afternoon, I was not busy and I helped sending out
chickens.
I wrote to Mr Abe and at 10pm, I went to bed.

March 8th 1935 (Friday)
From morning, it was mainly cloudy weather.
In the morning, I had done over 1,000 chickens.
It was not busy this afternoon.
I heard that Mr Nishitani arrived in London.
Today's hatchery, it was dull at the section of sexing chickens but it was busy at the sending out section that sent out 2,000 medium chickens. So I helped the sending out work.
At 5.30, I had tea and took a little rest.
Moribe visited me and went home soon.
At 7.30pm, Mrs Lumb brought a message that there will be job sexing chickens at Mr Kemp's for me.
It was considerable cold from this afternoon and truly nasty weather today.
When has come true spring? I can not wait for it!
Tonight, I went to bed early after taking a bath.

March 9th 1935 (Saturday)
This morning, I got up at 8am.
At 10am, I went to Mr Kemp to sex chickens.
It was very cold, an east strong wind and I felt that it went back again to winter.
From about 11am, I had done 320 chickens of Mr Kemp and 88 chickens of another persons.
After lunch, I got into bed for it was kept off the cold and slept till tea-time.
Terazawa called me and I got up.
After tea, I read a book in front of the fireplace.
It was strong wind, a chilly and nasty weather tonight.
It was too early to sleep for an afternoon nap.
I read a book to kill time.

March 10th 1935 (Sunday)
Since last night, it had been a strong wind and awfully cold outside this morning.
I could see from my bed that it was snowing through the window.
I was in no mood for getting up because it was cold in the morning.
I took breakfast on my bed.
It did not stop the wind afternoon, too. It was nasty weather.
I read a book by the fireplace and felt that it was long day today.
It was very cold day today, so every house's chimneys spewed out dense smoke all day.

March 11th 1935 (Monday)
It was very cold and a strong wind last night.
I couldn't stretch my legs in my bed for very cold.
This morning, it was good weather but it was a windy and cold.
In the morning, I had done over 500 chickens.
Afternoon, I helped that busy sending out of medium size chickens.
As a result of packing, I had a pain in my hands.
I received a letter from Mr Nishitani in London and the Society's Mr Kato and Mr Suzuki in Japan.
At 6pm, I took a tea and had a little rest.
I answered two letters to the Society.
At 1am I went to bed.

March 12th 1935 (Tuesday)
This morning, I got up at 8am and listened to the song of a bush warbler in my bed.

There was nothing only a scattered cloud in this morning sky.

It was beautiful weather unusually.

I had done above 1,300 chickens in the morning.

Afternoon, I ordered stamps from the office girl for two replies to Japan.

It was not busy my job and the chicken's boxes arrived, I helped to carry to up stair and packing. As a result, I had a pain in my hands today, too.

At 5.30pm, I had tea and a little rest in my lodging.

I wrote to my village headman and other few letters to Japan and I will post them tomorrow.

It was completely good weather today.

I went to bed after a bath.

March 13th 1935 (Wednesday)
This morning, I had slept till 11am and breakfast was on my bed.

Before lunch, I wrote a letter by the typewriter and the addresses of a few letters to Japan at the office.

By the way, I did my washing.

It was cloudy today compared with good weather yesterday.

I received a letter from Sugai and replied to him.

At about 2.30pm, I had done 77 chickens they were 'custom' [cross bred or pedigree?].

It used to be full darkness at that time 6pm before a little while but it was light still at same time today. I felt quite that it got longer hours of sunlight and the sun's position was raised.

At 5.30pm, I read a book until the tea.

Terazawa went to see Mr Thornber's house.

I went to bed early tonight.

March 14ᵗʰ 1935 (Thursday)
It was cloudy but comfortable day today.
In the morning, I had a lot of work but afternoon, I was dull.
Forwarding of chickens was busy so I helped a bit of packing.
Today's my records of discrimination was over 1,500 chickens.
At 6pm, I was back my lodging, tea and a little rest.
After bathing, I went to bed at about 10pm.

March 15ᵗʰ 1935 (Friday)
I went to work at 8.30am.
In the morning, it was a little bit busy but not busy afternoon.
Over 1,200 chickens were done.
As usual in the hatchery, it was busy to send out medium sized chickens.
At 6pm I went back my lodging and tea.
This afternoon, Mr Nishitani arrived and I went to see him with two others.
We visited Mr Thornber with four peoples.
Mr Thornber and Mr Nishitani had a talk in private.
So we spent a bit of time at the Thornber's office.
I was back at 8pm, a little rest and went to bed early.
It was a foggy day and nasty weather all day today.

March 16ᵗʰ 1935 (Saturday)
I took breakfast on my bed this morning, too.
At 10am, I visited Mr Nishitani in his lodging.
I carried Mr Nishitani's present from Mr Watson's house to Mr Lumb's house with Terazawa. The present was a set of coffee cups and saucers.
I killed time a little at the hatchery.

Mr Nishitani came and talked together with Mr Lumb.
At 1.50pm, Hattori and Taniguchi came and in the
afternoon we went to the town with six peoples. We took
tea at a hotel in the town.
Both, Hattori and Taniguchi stayed the hotel tonight.
Tomorrow, they are going to Liverpool so I am envious
of their visit.
I got back at 9pm and about 10pm, after bathing I went
to bed.

March 17th 1935 (Sunday)
At 8am, I got up and after breakfast I was waiting for
coming Taniguchi and Hattori.
At 9.20am, they came and we had chat with five peoples
at downstairs.
I saw them to Mr Watson's house.
At 10.30, I got back and after lunch, I was bored with
nothing to do.
I did napping, tea and reading.
Mr Nishitani came to see me and went back at 10pm.
I heard that management of the chicken hatchery trade
in England is a business in depression.
It is totally hopeless that entry into England from Japan
next year.[11]
Only I wish and pray to our safe working.
I get up with a hope and go to bed with thanks.
Be given happiness from God!
I will be in work tomorrow and went to bed at 10.30pm.

---

[11] In the introduction I mentioned the 'Spy Theory'. I think this
entry debunks that. Koichi sounds more like a man who is
more concerned about not having work in the future and not
expecting to come back to England due to the economic
depression rather than being withdrawn from active 'spy duty'
prior a declaration of war, which will be six years later.

March 18th 1935 (Monday)
At 7.30am, I got up.
In the morning, it was busy a little.
I had done over 1,200 chickens.
It was boring afternoon.
It was busy to send out medium chickens and I helped it.
I felt tired this afternoon for lack of sleep last night.
It was cloudy but warm today.
Tonight Nishitani and Moribe came to see me.

March 19th 1935 (Tuesday)
It was cloudy all day but I felt very warmly.
In the morning, I felt a little hot when I was at work.
I worked with keeping the door ajar because I felt to get dizzy for steam.
As usual, it was busy in the morning but afternoon, was a small number of chickens.
In total, I had done above 1,500 chickens.
It was busy with sending out of the medium chickens today, too.
I thought when I left my lodging that as usual it was boring this afternoon but everyone were working with a busy look. I could not reading and I helped packing of sending out.
At 5.30pm, I got the owner's signature and after tea, I went to buy cigarettes.
I could see very good moon and got sentimental, it was a spring night with a hazy moon.
Unfortunately, the station shop was closed and I made a circuit of the town.
I got back hastily.
It was very warm tonight, too but I regretted that I couldn't see the sun still.
I was waiting impatiently for I would set foot in Japan.

It is a holiday tomorrow and I will read a magazine.
Moribe came to see me.

March 20th 1935 (Wednesday)
I took breakfast on my bed at about 9.30am, got up at
10am and read a book in the morning.
After lunch, I visited Mr Nishitani and stayed for a little
while.
I climbed a hill at the back with Terazawa from about
2pm to 3.30pm.
Suitable for springtime, a skylark was heard singing.
We went to the hatchery to be idle.
The hatchery was busy with sending out of 2,000
medium chickens and I helped it a little.
I wrote a postal card to my brother.
After tea, Mr Nishitani came to see me. He said to me
that he would visit Mr Lumb tonight.
And I read a book.
I could see the sun from this morning and it was good
and warm weather day all day to day.
I went to bed early after took a bath.

March 21st 1935 (Thursday)
It was cloudy but warm.
They said that in England, it starts spring season from
today.
It was very busy my job the whole day and I had done
over 1,400.
I saw Mr Nishitani to the station and he said he would
visit Mr Spink and go here and there.
At 5.30pm, I got the owner's signature and 6pm, tea and
a little rest.
As always in the hatchery, it was busy with the medium
chickens.

I went to bed early tonight.

March 22nd 1935 (Friday)
At 7.30am, I got up and washed my face and shaved myself in passing.
After breakfast 8.20am, I went to work and it was a little bit busy.
I had done over 1,500 chickens.
It was good weather from morning. At about 4pm it was rainfall but soon fine again.
Scattered clouds were drifting in the sky to the east.
After diner at 5.30pm, Moribe came to see me and he talked about his love affairs.[12]
I heard it.
I was waiting for a letter from my country every day but nothing today.
I became fed up with it.
I heard that we could receive spending money from Mr Nishitani from today.

March 23rd 1935 (Saturday)
It was a heavy fall of rain last night and a rainfall today, too.

---

[12] It is hard to believe that this would fit the idea of a western type love affair. [Unless he found romance in the valley, Yorkshire style?] As mentioned above most Japanese marriages were arranged and romance was not the glue in the marriage. Many men who could afford it had mistresses without any social stigmas to him or his wife. It is unlikely that there would have been significant available women for Moribe to make the story a long one! It is said that the Japanese don't have the same moral codes as the in West but they do have a sense of the right and wrong time or place for such things. Koichi does not seem overly impressed anyhow!

At about 9am, I had breakfast on my bed.

Moribe came to see me and I went to a barber's shop with him.

The charge was 8 pence and an extra was expensive 2 pence. *[Hair oils, perhaps?]*

Before lunch, Itoh came to see me and I had lunch with him.

Afternoon, Moribe came to see us and we talked with four peoples.

I heard that they held the conference of hatcheries.

It was nasty and rainy weather today.

March 24th 1935 (Sunday)

I slept till 9am and at about 9.30am, after washed my face, I took a breakfast.

In the morning, it was strong wind and threatening to rain.

It was mainly cloudy and foul weather today the whole day.

I read the magazine, 'Fuji' and I was bored by tedium for long day on Sunday.

Afternoon, from 2pm, I went to walk with Moribe and Terazawa to a hill at the house back.

Afternoon, I could see the sun a little but it was mainly cloudy weather.

I got back my lodging at 3.30pm and I read a book until tea.

I was disappointed by food that was served, a kind of cold confectionery every once a week.

I could not get a feeling of fullness by that food.

I slept again until 9pm and took a bath.

March 25th 1935 (Monday - *Koichi's Birthday*)
I couldn't sleep well last night, dozed away until 3.30am
and fell asleep.
This morning, I was woken by the landlady and went to
work.
In the morning a little busy and afternoon, I helped
sending out of the medium chickens.
I had done over 1,400.
In the morning, I was hard to see and I hesitated over
my decisions a little.
But my eyesight got well gradually again. That cause
was probably two consecutive holidays.
The sun shone a little bit in the morning.
At 5.30pm, I had tea and at that time it looked like rain.
Terazawa came to see me. I went to bed early tonight.

March 26th 1935 (Tuesday)
It was fine weather this morning.
I did gradually my work and afternoon, I had similar
nothing to do.
It was much the same as no job.
I had done over 1,400 in a day.
At 5pm, Terazawa came to see me and at 6pm, tea and a
little rest.
It was fine and sometimes cloudy weather and a strong
wind.
When I went out of doors I felt coldness.

March 27th 1935 (Wednesday)
At 9am, I got up and went to work at 10am.
I had done about 200 chickens.
I went back my lodging at once and it was good weather
suitable for spring.

In the morning, I visited Mr Lumb's house for a moment and read a book with got sunshine at back site of the lodging.

After lunch, I went to buy cigarettes, on my way there I got the catalogue at the office and I sent it to Hattori.

It was very good that was fine weather.

I imagined that a bud of cherry blossoms grew larger in Japan.

[Cherry Blossom time in Japan is a major festival and celebration time.]

Afternoon, when I stopped at the hatchery, it was very busy sending out of medium chickens.

The hatchery bought 'sex-link'[13] of medium chickens from Mr Thornber and sent out.

Moribe came to see me but I learned nothing from him today.

March 28th 1935 (Thursday)

It was warm and comfortable day the whole day.

In the morning, it was busy a little and I had done over 2,100 chickens.

I received letters from Mr Kojima, Ochiai farm of the training school and Mr Okawa.

This evening, Moribe came to see me and I wrote a letter.

It was my birthday on March 25th. I was given one pack of 50 cigarettes called Gold Flake from Mrs Lumb in celebration of my birthday.

March 29th 1935 (Friday)

At 7.30, I got up and went to work.

---

[13] Sex-Linked Chickens are cross breeds e.g. Brown Leghorn Cockerels mated to White Wyandotte Hens. They are more difficult to sex as chicks so only 90% of any batch was guaranteed to farmers.

I thanked Mrs Lumb for her birthday present to me yesterday.

I've been busy in the morning and I had done over 2,000 chickens.

At 5.30pm, I went back for tea.

After tea, Mr Nishitani and Mr Moribe came to see me.

I received spending money, one pound.

I wrote answered a letter Mr Saburo Kojima [Sister's brother-in-law].

It was a rainfall this afternoon.

The clock stroked 11pm when I was writing the Ochiai Farm a letter.

At once I went to bed.

March 30th 1935 (Saturday)

It was rain from this morning.

At about 9am, I had breakfast on my bed and got up at 10am.

It stopped rain at that time.

In the morning, I wrote letters and after lunch, Mr Nishitani and Mr Moribe came to see me. We talked together till 3.30pm and went to a manager's house of Mr Watson.

We were idle a little time and made a circuit of the town and went back at 5pm.

We met Mr and Mrs Lumb by chance in the town and they drove a car.

At the post office, I bought four picture postcards and a stamp book that the price was 2 shilling. And wrote a letter again.

After tea, We went to a movie with four peoples.

I got back at 8.30pm from the movie and at 10pm, bathing.

I went to bed at 11pm.

March 31th 1935 (Sunday)
At about 10am, as always I had breakfast on my bed and
read a book.
I fell into a doze and the landlady informed me of
lunchtime but I didn't get up in the end.
I skipped my lunch once.
At 1.30pm, I got up and visited Mr Nishitani.
After went back, I read a book till tea time.
I sent a letter that enclosed a picture postcard to my
brother, Shunji.
I posted the letter at 6pm.
It was nasty weather and threatening to rain.
Mr Nishitani came to see me after tea.
We read a book together three peoples.
We stopped to chat with three peoples at 9pm.
Mr Nishitani went back and I went to bed at 11pm but I
couldn't sleep for were wakeful.

April 1st 1935 (Monday)
This morning, I woke up at 6.30am and it was too early
to get up.
I had short sleep again and just 8am, jumped out of bed.
I went to work at 8.20am.
It was mainly cloudy and nasty weather.
It was busy a little in the morning but afternoon, not
busy.
It was busy sending out of about 400 medium chickens
in the hatchery.
I helped it.
I had done over 2,000 chickens in the whole day today.
Hattori came to see me on his way his lodging from the
hatchery.
In the evening, Mr Nishitani came to see me.

I received the magazine, the March number of 'The Domestic Fowl World' from Japan.
It was a rainfall off and on when after tea. Reading, Bathing and early went to bed.

April 2nd 1935 (Tuesday)
It bathed in the sunshine on my bed from about 6am.
I got up at 8am, made preparations for attendance and I went to work.
It was busy in the morning and I had done about 2,100 today, too.
It was mainly cloudy weather and cold day.
At 6pm, after tea, I went to shopping to the town with Terazawa but unfortunately, each shop was closed. We went back in vain and I parted with him. I stopped at Mr Watson's house.
On my way lodging, I met Mr Nishitani by chance.
Moribe came to see me and I talked with him.

April 3rd 1935 (Wednesday)
At 8am, I got up and I saw Terazawa on to the train at 9.06am. [He was going home to Japan.]
It was fine and sometimes cloudy weather and cold.
On the way to see Terazawa, I went to the hatchery.
It was holiday today but I had worked a little. I had done about 1,000 included afternoon.
At 3pm, I got back my lodging and went to buy cigarettes.
I read a book again and was bored with it. I was left alone from today.
When I longed for my home country, I felt tears welling up in my eyes with painful sentiment.
I felt that even every day's meal. I had no appetite by a strong longing for memories.

I read a book again and Moribe came to see me and talked together.

After bathing, I went to bed early.

It was cold weather today.

April 4th 1935 (Thursday)

The landlady woke me up this morning.

At 8am, I made arrangements and went to work.

It was good weather but considerably cold and I saw a snowfall in the daytime.

I had done over 2,000.

At 6pm, after tea, I wrote Terazawa the first letter to Marseilles.

And incidentally, I wrote to my home.

It seemed outside, considerably cold and a windy, too.

I read a book and went to bed early.

April 5th 1935 (Friday)

I got up at 7.30am and looked at the sunshine. It was good day.

Unusually, it was not busy my job in the morning and busy afternoon.

I had done over 2,600.

I was surprised that it was a snowfall at noon and tremendous snow.

At 6pm, after tea, Mr Nishitani came to see me.

Until about 10pm, I heard his life story.

After bathing, I went to bed early tonight, too.

April 6th 1935 (Saturday)

Last night, it was a strong wind and cold night.

At 8am, I got up and in the morning, I had done about 400.

When I was idle, Itoh came. I heard they held the meeting of hatcheries at Mr Thornber's
Afternoon, I had a talk with Mr Nishitani and others, four peoples.
At 2pm, Itoh went back.
It was fine weather but a little slightly cold.
I washed my face afternoon and I intend that will go to the cinema this evening.
I was glad that it became gradually to be warm.
I received the letters from Tadaichi [Brother] and Aunt Ikeda and replied to that letters and others.

April 7th 1935 (Sunday)
It was a rainfall from this morning.
At about 9am, the landlady carried my breakfast to my bed and I had eaten it on my bed.
In the morning, I read a book on there and had a short sleep.
I got up at 12.30pm and after lunch, I read a book again.
After tea, Mr Nishitani came to see me and talked together.
I didn't know why, Moribe hadn't come to see me today.
We engaged in a heated discussion just with two peoples.
After bathing, I went to bed early.

April 8th 1935 (Monday)
At 8am, I got up with the landlady got me up and I went to work at 8.30am.
I was busy in this morning and annoyed by young Lorrie.
I had done over 2,500.
After tea, Mr Nishitani and Moribe came to see me and we talked together.

Today, I received the bulletin of the association's branch from my home, from an unknown sender with the envelope that I sent. Probably, it was from Saburo Kojima [Sister's brother-in-law].
I went to bed early tonight, too.

April 9th 1935 (Tuesday)
It was warm weather today the whole day.
I had done over 2,300.
At 5.30pm, after tea, I wrote a letter. Mr Nishitani and Moribe went to the cinema.
At night, I went out to post in the rain.
I forwarded Terazawa's letter for him to Napoli.
After bathing, I went to bed early tonight too.

April 10th 1935 (Wednesday)
I went to work at about 9am and in the morning, I had done about 600 chickens.
Mr Nishitani came to Mr Lumb's house to make a check the records and make adjustment.
I went back my lodging with him and after lunch, we visited Mr Thornber.
I helped a little and I had done special white leghorns breed, about 100 chickens.
I had a headache for the testing room's temperature was too warm.
The result of sexing chickens today, there were lots of females and I re-checked.
I had made too many mistakes and was disheartened about it.

Only I pray to God that I can perform my responsibility without accident.[14]

After tea, I went to bed early for tomorrow working.

April 11th 1935 (Thursday)
I was busy all day and it was a strong wind but fine weather.

After tea, there were sexing chickens a little and I had done a little with the help Mr Nishitani and Moribe. At 8.30pm, we returned and took supper together.

At 10pm, bathing and went to bed.

April 12th 1935 (Friday)
It was good weather and worthy of spring.

At about 4pm Mr Nishitani came to see me and he helped my job about 100 chickens.

Moribe stopped at the hatchery on his way home.

At 5pm, we went back with three companies.

Mr Nishitani brought the payment for lodging and spending money for me.

It will be holiday tomorrow so we talked together and I went to bed at 10pm.

April 13th 1935 (Saturday)
It was fine weather.

I had breakfast on my bed and slept again.

I got up at noon. After lunch, we played cards with three peoples.

Brother of Moribe's landlord [a Watson] had visited my lodging with his wife and a child.

When tea time, I had my photograph taken by him.

---

[14] Another example as to just how important doing a quality job was to Koichi's pride and self-confidence.

I started to write the letter to my friend but for the present, interrupted it and went to the town to stroll.
This evening, I went to the cinema with Moribe from 9pm.
I got back at a little before 11pm.

April 14th 1935 (Sunday)
I slept in my bed with like dozing off.
I had breakfast on my bed at about 9am as always.
Miserably, I was reading a novel while I need to go to the toilet and at about 11am, I got up for relief and I slept again.
At about 1pm Mr Nishitani came to see me and he got me up.
At once, I jumped out of bed and had lunch.
Afternoon, I played cards and at night, played cards again at Mr Nishitani's house *[Slater Greenwood's home, 66 Palace House Road]*.
I was treated for supper and got back and went to bed at 11pm.

April 15th 1935 (Monday)
It was a misty morning and a foggy whole day today.
Work was slack but I had done over 2,800.
At 6pm, after tea, I wrote to Sueo Osada *[old school friend]*.
Moribe and Mr Nishitani came to see me but soon they had to get back.
At 8.30pm, when we were talking, Mr Lumb came for me because there was work. I sexed chickens over 300 chickens.
At 10pm I took a bath and went to bed.

April 16th 1935 (Tuesday)
It was rainy weather this morning, too.
On the way to work, I posted the reply to my friend
Osada.
I was busy the whole day and I had done over 3,200.
At 6pm I took tea and a rest.
It became good weather but it was as usual a cloudy sky.
It was light until 9pm and I went to bed early tonight,
too.

April 17th 1935 (Wednesday)
At 8am, I got up. It was a rainfall.
I went to work at 9am and from about 10am, had done
about 1,200.
Mr Nishitani came to pay a bill.
Afternoon, I was going to go to help Moribe but I had
bad headache so I put off to go.
At about 3pm I heard that there were 250 chickens of
special breed and I went to the hatchery in the rain.
I got back at 4.30pm and tea. My bad headache was
unchanged.
I put off bathing and went to bed early.

I had a spot by the side of my
lip, weighed on my mind and
had a slight cold.

April 18th 1935 (Thursday)
It was good weather today.
I could not sleep and was
uncomfortable from 2am to
about 5am, it reason was I
went to bed early last night.
I had done over 3,400 with
Moribe's help until 3.30pm. I
received his help all day.

*We did it! 3,400
chicks sexed!*

86

I went back my lodging but they were out and I went to Moribe's lodging.

After tea, I reply the letter to a friend, Suzuki and wrote to my brother, Shunji and posted.

Moribe came to see me later.

April 19th 1935 (Friday)

It was mainly cloudy weather today.

I was busy this morning.

I finished my work about 2pm. I had done over 2,000.

My head felt heavy and felt dizzy for had a cold.

Half of the workers from the hatchery took a holiday this afternoon because of it was 'nice Friday' [Good Friday].

I helped with the incubator's job, until about 3.30pm.

I didn't take a bath tonight.

Got dressed up to go to the cinema tonight but unfortunately, we couldn't get in because the tickets were all sold in advance.

I got back at 11pm and went straight to bed.

April 20th 1935 (Saturday)

The weather was rainfall this morning.

As usual, I had breakfast and I got up at 11am.

I wrote a letter to my sister.

From afternoon, my hosts of lodgings went to shopping to Leeds all together and they were away from home.

I went to buy stamps to the post office with Moribe and we made a circuit of the north side in the town.

At about 3.30pm, we got back and I read a book.

I was treated to afternoon tea together at Moribe's lodgings.

The weather was nasty rainfall afternoon too.

I took supper with landlord and wife at about 8pm.

They said to me that Mr Nishitani and they got back together by same train.

I felt truly a longing for Japan.
I went to bed at 10pm.

April 21st 1935 (Sunday)
The weather was fine in the morning.
As usual, I had breakfast on my bed and 11am, got up.
A little while till lunchtime, I read a newspaper.
Afternoon, I made a circuit of a hill at the back with
Moribe and we visited Mr Nishitani.
I played cards with the boss of Nishitani's house, Mr
Greenwood.[15]
I got back for afternoon tea.
This evening, Nishitani and
Moribe came to see me and
we wrote the request for to
make procedural document
of our consulate.
We talked together about
many things and they left
together sometime after
9pm. I went to bed at about 10pm.

April 22nd 1935 (Monday)

From this morning, it was suitable weather for spring.
Easter holiday, I was busy in the morning but it was like
a holiday in the afternoon.
I had intended to help Moribe's work afternoon but I
had to check a small number of chickens.
At about 3pm, my work had finished.

---

[15] Slater Greenwood died on 18th May 1935. Mr Nishitani
[Mitsuo] had a flower urn placed on the grave inscribed 'Sweet
Memories, Mitsuo'. This can still be seen today at Slack Top
cemetery, Heptonstall.

Mrs Lumb took Donald's[16] girlfriend [*Renée Wilcock*] to the hatchery. She was a beauty. She was 19 years old and very pretty.

Renée Wilcock. 'She was a beauty'!

After that I talked with Donald's girlfriend and Mrs Lumb, altogether four peoples for a little bit time. Today's newspaper said an earthquake happened in Taiwan. *[3000 died.]*

---

[16] Donald Sutcliffe – Nephew to Thomas & Amy Lumb.

I got back at about 4.30pm, after afternoon tea, Mr Nishitani came to see me and Moribe came later than him.

At about 8.30pm, I had a shave and took a little rest.

I got well my cold but would withhold a bath two or three days.

Today was Monday, but I couldn't receive even one letter and felt lonely.

I would like to go to bed early again tonight.

Now, it is quarter to nine but it is still light.

April 23rd 1935 (Tuesday)
Today was the last day of Easter holiday. All the workers in the hatchery had done their best work. The work, sexing chickens finished in the morning and I had done over 100 chickens in the afternoon.

Two office workers helped to check the eggs and to return into the incubator.

Afternoon, I was busy and until at about 3.30pm, I helped to send out the medium chickens.

All the newborn chickens had been sent out in the morning.

I got back my lodging at 4pm and read a book until afternoon tea.

Tonight, I played cards in my room with Mr Nishitani and Moribe until about 9pm.

At 10pm, bathing and at about 11pm went to bed.

I could receive letter nothing for me.

A letter from Japan addressed to Hattori was received c/o Mr Lumb and I forwarded it to him.

April 24th 1935 (Wednesday)
Today was mainly cloudy but it was a warm day.

I worked by myself because of that it was busy to send out 3,000 medium chickens.

I was very busy today. I had to send out 3,000 medium chickens, all on my own.

I was busy in the morning but in the afternoon, I had done small number of chickens.

My work finished at about 2pm and I helped to send out the medium chickens.

At 6pm, after tea, I was waiting with Moribe for Donald to come but, he didn't arrive.

We promised to meet and to go for social evening tonight. He made a mistake and forgot us.

From about 8pm, I went to buy cigarettes with Moribe. We visited Mr Lumb's home and played cards until at about 11pm.

I went home to bed after 11pm.

April 25th 1935 (Thursday)
Today was mainly cloudy but good weather.

I was busy the whole day today and I had done over 2,700 chickens.

I reccived the letters from Chiyoko [*sister*] and my uncle. After, afternoon tea, I went to a barber's shop with Moribe.

I got back at 8pm, I wrote the reply to Chiyoko.

It was a strong wind and cold out of doors.

Mr Nishitani visited Itoh yesterday and returned today.

I put off to write till tomorrow reply to my uncle and I took a bath and went to bed.

April 26th 1935 (Friday)
The clear and cloudless sky, I wished for! This weather that 'complete British clear weather', no it was

'European clear weather', it was good weather day today.[17]

I had done over 2,700 chickens.

I enjoyed myself with Nishitani and Moribe.

I received a letter from Sugano.

I went to bed early.

April 27th 1935 (Saturday)

As usual, I had breakfast in bed and I got up at about 9.30am.

I went to the hatchery to kill time and I stayed there for about one hour.

After this I went home.

After lunch, I wrote a reply to my uncle.

From about 2pm, I played cards at Mr Nishitani's place.

From about at 4pm, I took a walk with Moribe and returned there at 5pm.

I read a book whilst waiting for afternoon tea.

In this morning, Mr Nishitani arranged our wages, I heard.

From this morning, it was good weather today for but I felt slightly cold.

I went to the cinema. After this I went home at about 11pm and went to bed.

Always, 'the second house' in Saturday was full of people.

April 28th 1935 (Sunday)

As usual, I had breakfast in bed and I got up at about 10am, after that I took a bath.

------

[17] Koichi was excited by the blue sky when saying 'British clear weather' – in the Japanese text he was referring to an old traditional saying 'Nippon Bare' meaning 'Japanese clear sky'.

I took a walk alone and I met Mrs Lumb on the way and so I called in at her house.

I was taken by Mr and Mrs Lumb over to Blackpool.

We started at 1pm, together five peoples, and we arrived there at 3pm.

We enjoyed ourselves there until 6.30pm and got back at 8.30pm.

It was a round trip of 110 miles. It was very fine weather and so I felt good.

It was very crowded there and many cars formed a line. *[Traffic Jam!]*

After we came back, I was treated some wine at Mr Lumb's house. I left at about 9pm.

April 29th 1935 (Monday)

I was tired extremely, it was caused by the yesterday's drive.

I was woken up by my landlady this morning.

It was lovely weather today.

I was busy in the morning. I had done over 2,500 chickens.

The Society and Tadaichi *[brother]* sent me the magazine 'Hinode' *[Sunrise]* and a letter today.

At night, I wrote the reply to Tadaichi and I went to bed early.

April 30th 1935 (Tuesday)

Today was cloudy but it was a good weather.

I was busy the whole day and I had done over 3,000 chickens.

In the evening, Hattori and Taniguchi stopped at the hatchery with Mr Nishitani.

I immediately finished my work and I went back to my lodging with them.

We drank afternoon tea together.

The colour of the clouds looked like rain.

I played cards with Mr Nishitani, Moribe, Hattori and Taniguchi until about 10pm.

It was late, two of my friends decided to stay the night because they could not get home.

May 1st 1935 (Wednesday)

I got up at 8am and I saw two people off at 9am.

Today was slightly cold with nasty weather.

At the hatchery and Mr Lumb's house, I relaxed for a short time.

I took a nap from at 11am to 1.30pm.

In the afternoon, I checked over 1,300 chickens.

I dropped in at Mr Lumb's house and after afternoon tea I visited there again with Moribe.

Mrs Lumb, Moribe and I went to the cake shop which Mrs Lumb's sister ran. *[In Holme Street, currently Max's Jewellers. The sister was Minnie Sutcliffe, nee Hirst.]*

On the way home, we went to Donald's house and we played cards until about at 10pm. Donald said that his two housemaids went to the cinema tonight.

He went to bed at 11pm. I was surprised that the housemaids were off duty and the master *[Mr Lumb]* came for milk instead of his housemaid.[18]

I had met Mr Lumb as he came for milk on his way and I went back with him.

I admire him, he worked very hard.

Mr Nishitani went on a business trip to Kent and he would return next week.

---

[18] Another culture shock! Women, including wives, in Japan would never have been 'off duty'.

94

May 2nd 1935 (Thursday)
Today was mainly cloudy but it was a warm day.
I was busy in the morning.
I received a letter that was written by Tadaichi [brother]
from my home.
I checked over 2,700 chickens and after afternoon tea I
wrote the reply.
I went for a walk alone and stopped at the hatchery to
kill time.
I saw the Jubilee Day's flag[19] on the hatchery's roof.
I went to bed early tonight again.

May 3rd 1935 (Friday)
As usual, today was mainly cloudy but it was a very
warm day.
Today was Moribe's day off and he helped my work all
day.
We checked over 5,000 chickens.
We finished our work at about 4pm and we took a
walked together.
The housemaid said Mr and Mrs Lumb went to Mr
Joys's house.
We had a chat with her a little time.
We returned my lodging.
I went to bed early as usual.

May 4th 1935 (Saturday)
Today was a warm and a good weather.
I got up at 10am and I went for a walk with Moribe.
We dropped in at Mr Lumb's house and we played table
tennis at the hatchery till lunch.

---

[19] These flags were in preparation for the Silver Jubilee of King
George V to be celebrated on May 6th that year.

I received a letter from Mr Nishitani.

After afternoon tea, I took a walk to the north area in the town with Moribe again.

We met Ernest's and Donald's parents by chance and I bought some cigarettes.

I returned home at 7.30pm and read a magazine.

In the town, now that the Imperial Silver Jubilee is just around corner on next Monday and 'Flag raising' was very beautiful.

There was no a bath tonight and I went to bed 10pm.

May 5th 1935 (Sunday)

The weather was more springlike and I could see only a peace of scattered clouds in the sky from this morning.

At 10am, after breakfast I took a stroll.

The wind was not bitterly cold but a refreshing breeze in spring.

I had lunch at 3pm for my breakfast was at 10am.

Until it, I took a walk on the hill at the back of my lodging with Moribe.

After lunch, I took a nap until 8pm and I washed my face.

It was light still at 9pm.

I heard about my tomorrow work's plan from Mr Lumb on the way to take a walk.

He said that tomorrow is the holiday for the Silver Jubilee.

May 6th 1935 (Monday)

Today is the British Imperial Silver Jubilee the day and a public holiday.

From in the morning, we had fine weather and fine today.

I had breakfast on my bed at 9am and I got up at 10am.

I went to help to the Thornber's hatchery and Moribe's number of the contract was finished all with my help over 300 chickens in the morning

I got back home about at 2pm and I had lunch.

I went to listen to the brass band the square in front of Watson's Hatchery.

There was very crowded with good weather.

I visited Mr Lumb when he was on the point of going out with his wife and her sister.

I had afternoon tea at 6pm. Although hot water was cold, I had a bath.

I took a walk to the town and strolled in the town from about 7pm.

The town was crowded with people from 9pm and I happened to meet the master and Donald.

At 9.25pm, after a man [Coun, R A Parker – Chairman of the Council] made a speech, the blinking lights he turn on the bridge.

And I went to Bonfire on the hill with Donald.

I got back home at about 11pm and I went to bed.

The 'Blinking Lights' on the old Packhorse Bridge

May 7ᵗʰ 1935 (Tuesday)
Today was good weather and I checked over 4,700
chickens, I obtain help from Moribe.
The hatchery was busy for sending off the medium sized
chickens so I helped them a little.
After afternoon tea, I washed my face and took a walk
but I gave up halfway because strong wind.
I visited Mr Lumb's house but Mrs Lumb was on the
point of going out to attend a party of card playing.
I got back my lodging and I took a little rest.
At about 7pm, Mr Nishitani got back here from his
business trip.
We talked together with three people until about 10pm.
I expect that perhaps, I can return home with Moribe.

May 8ᵗʰ 1935 (Wednesday)
In the morning, I checked over 2,000 chickens and in the
afternoon, I had rest.
I wrote Shunji *[youngest brother]* a letter and I posted it by
the afternoon mail.
At about 4pm, I have a little work to check.
After afternoon tea, I went to shopping to the town with
Moribe.
At about 7pm, we visited Donald's with Mrs Lumb and
we played cards until about 10pm.
Mr Lumb took us home back with him by his car and I
was treated to supper.
I returned my lodging at 10.30pm and I went to bed at
11pm.
I could see a good half moon in the west sky. I mustn't
get too sentimental.
I heard that it was busy my tomorrow work.
Donald's fiancée is a really beauty! *[Second time of
mentioning this fact!]*

May 9th 1935 (Thursday)

In the morning, it was cold but in the afternoon it got warm.

I received the letters from Shunji and Mr Takabatake and I replied them.

I checked over about 5,000 chickens for a day's work.

After afternoon tea, I was busy with two replies.

From about 8pm, I went to buy cigarettes and on the way to there, I stopped at the hatchery.

I idled away my time there and the night workers for egg checking were working busily.

I went to bed at 10.30pm.

May 10th 1935 (Friday)

I was busy in the morning but in the afternoon, it was slow.

I check about over 4,000 chickens. But could have do 9,000.

From last night, it was a strong wind and the weather was fine today but a little cold outside.

I visited Mr Lumb's house tonight and I played cards until about at 10pm and I was treated to supper.

I went to bed 11.30pm.

May 11th 1935 (Saturday)

At about 8.30am, Moribe came for me, I jumped out of bed at once and I ate breakfast.

I went to call on the Thornber's hatchery to pay my thanks.

I met Mr Nishitani and I got back home with him and after lunch we visited Mr Watson's house together three people. We had our souvenir photograph taken there.

Back L-R: Willy Watson & Ernest Wood.
Front L-R: Moribe, Nishitani & Koichi Andoh.

From about 4.30pm, at Mr Greenwood's, Nishitani and
Moribe played Hanahuda *[Japanese card game, Hanahuda
means flower cards]* and I played cards a little time.
After afternoon tea, when we were talking together
Donald came for us and his fiancée, Renée. Moribe and I
had stylishly a drive to Keighley together four people.
We run and run by car and I was surprised that her
driving was pretty skilful.[20]
They took me home in his car and I had a chat with
husband and wife of my lodging till at 11.30pm. I went
to bed at midnight.

---

[20] Another culture shock! - Women drivers in 1930s Japan? Not
likely!

A day out. A 'Stylishly drive'! Koichi & Moribe with Donald and Renée. ['She is a really beauty'!]

May 12th 1935 (Sunday)

Today was my last Sunday.

As usual, I had breakfast on my bed.

I wrote to my friends who I got to know during my stay in England.

In the afternoon, I went to post office to post them with Moribe.

On my way home I dropped in at Mr Nishitani's and we played Japanese playing cards a little.

Today, I wrote to Itoh, Mr Kuno, Kumei and Mr Ikuta, four people.
In the morning, I arranged the interior of my suitcase.
After afternoon tea, we took a walk together three people.
We walked and walked a very much of walking today.
I took a bath at 10pm and I went to bed at about 10.30pm.

May 13th 1935 (Monday)
Today was not so busy and in the afternoon I was bored.
At about 3pm, I got back my lodging and I went to the town to the barber's and to buy a wallet. The barber's trimmed in a disorderly ability therefore I felt itchy very much.
At once, I returned home and I washed my hair.
After that, I visited Mr Lumb's house and I talked together.
After I got back my lodging, I talked with Moribe until about 11pm.
It was cloudy weather and bad in the open air.

May 14th 1935 (Tuesday)
It was my last day in England today.
At 5pm, Taniguchi came to see me with Hattori.
After afternoon tea, I went to Mr Watson's and Mr Lumb's house to call on them to pay my respects and thanks for their kindness during my stay in England.
About 10pm, I got back and I went to bed but I couldn't fall asleep easily.
Today was cloudy weather and slightly cold.

May 15th 1935 (Wednesday)
I woke up at 6am and today was good weather.

I was busy with preparations of leaving for home.

I was unwilling to part from the hatchery's master, his wife and other staff.

Mr and Mrs Lumb sent off me to the station.

I also parted from Hattori.

I started home from Hebden Bridge by the 9.06am train.

Cora Ward

The office worker Miss Cora gave me the present as my girlfriend.

I arrived at the Kibworth station at after 1pm and I idled away my time until 3.30pm.

I met Sugano and Takabatake after a long interval.

Colleagues at Kibworth Hatchery, Leicestershire.

103

I left for London at 3.36pm and I arrived at 7.07pm.
At about 8pm, I ate dinner at Hinodeya *[Japanese hotel in London]*.
I took a walk together four people.
I went to bed at 11pm.

May 16th 1935 (Thursday)
I got up at 9am, and I had breakfast.
In the morning, I did my shopping at Asakami *[Japanese store in London?]* and I stopped at Tokiwa *[Japanese restaurant in London]*. I was waiting Mr Nishitani there but he hadn't come.
We got back to our hotel together three people.
After lunch, our three people went to walk a little time.
At 3pm, we started from the hotel by taxi to Fenchurch Street Station.
And we left for Royal Albert Dock from Fenchurch Street Station.
At last, I left for my home country.
I got aboard on the mail steamer the SS *Hakusan Maru*, it took about one hour. *[The ship he had arrived on belonging to the Japan Yusen Company.]*
I ate dinner at 6pm and I took a little rest.
At about 8pm, Mr Ikuta came to see me and he left the ship at 10pm.
A little time later the ship would set sail for Japan.
Sleeping was difficult on different bed. I dozed as I greeted the dawn.

May 17th 1935 (Friday)
It was a calm wave on the sea.
I had Japanese style breakfast. Nice I got the Japanese taste again.
I had a sleepless tonight for I had taken a nap.

I felt hard pitching and rolling on the ship because of we might have come near Bay of Biscay. The ship went fell behind about for thirty minutes tonight.

A sea from wave entered by the window in my room.

May 18th 1935 (Saturday)

The weather was good but a wave was big and pitching and rolling were hard.

The ship went fell behind about for thirty minute tonight again.

I didn't take breakfast for I got up late.

In the morning, pitching and rolling were hard but in the afternoon, they were put down.

I heard that the ship would pass through Bay of Biscay early tonight.

I played cards and listened to music by the gramophone.

I went to bed early.

May 19th 1935 (Sunday)

This morning, weather was good and a quiet morning.

Our vessel didn't pitch and roll and it was a good voyage's weather.

I wrote to the association, Mr Suzuki and Kato, the chief Yamaguchi, my firm chief at Inagaki, Tadaichi [brother], Mr Nishitani and Mr Ikuta.

I watched the cinema on the deck and after I played cards with Moribe.

Moribe lost so treated me to two bottle of beers.

I ate dinner at 5pm and after that I had a chat with others.

May 20th 1935 (Monday)

It was a quite calm voyage and cloudy.

After dinner, I played cards with Moribe and I lost the game tonight.

I treated him to two bottles of beer.
I talked with a cabin boy.
It looked like rain and it was strong wind but the ship didn't pitch and roll.

May 21st 1935 (Tuesday)
Last night, I had a pleasant chat with my colleagues in my cabin until about 1am.
It was a rainy weather and I could see Gibraltar.
At 6am, I got up and I washed my face and I was waiting for breakfast.
There was a big waves and the ship repeated the strong pitching and rolling.
Moribe bought a big octopus and we ate it at lunch and dinner, too.
It was good weather and weather for voyage.
At about 9am, the ship entered port in Gibraltar and set sail from there at noon.
From evening, it looked as if we were going to have a storm.
I treated Moribe to bottles of beer for I lost the cards game tonight again.
I wrote to three relatives Higashitanaka, Komatsuji and Ikeda in Nagoya.

May 22nd 1935 (Wednesday)
From morning, pitching and rolling of our ship was violent.
I felt sick very much.
I didn't eat dinner this evening and I was nonplussed.
It became the night but the strong wind and pitching and rolling didn't stop.
I guess, I fell asleep barely from about 1am.

May 23rd 1935 (Thursday)
The voyage was calm in this morning.
I got a letter from my uncle that my maternal
grandfather had died.
At once, I sent the letter of condolence.
I heard that our steamer would enter Marseilles Port at
7pm this evening.
After enter port, I looked round the in the city and I
returned at midnight.
It was exchange rate of 73 franc to the English pound.
And I went to bed.

May 24th 1935 (Friday)
After breakfast, we went to see the city sights together
three companies.
Moribe did not get back to the ship yet.
It was not hot and cold, and the weather was good.
At 5.30pm the departure gong sounded and we parted
from Marseilles.
It was an erotic town and I disliked there.
The steamer headed straight for Napoli in Italy.

May 25th 1935 (Saturday)
I got up at 7am and it was quite calm voyage.
I wrote to Itoh, Hattori, Sugano, Takabatake, Kuno,
Kumei and Shunji [brother].
I lost a play cards tonight again and I treated the
opponents to two bottles of beer.
I chatted with colleagues until 10pm in the hall.
I went to bed about at 11pm and our vessel didn't pitch
and roll.
Sea was calm.

May 26th 1935 (Sunday)
This morning at 7am, the steamer entered Napoli in
Italy.
After anchorage, I got up and I had breakfast.
And then I went ashore and as usual I looked round in
the town.
I saw the Pompeii Dance and the charge was half a
crown in English currency.
At 10am, I went back to the ship and I took a little rest.
I received a letter from Mr Nishitani today.
At 3pm, our ship left Napoli for Port Said.
After dinner, I wrote Chiyoko *[sister]* a letter.
From today, my cabin became fifth berth room.
This morning, the passenger of next room lost money
[stolen?] and the whole ship was in utter confusion
[searched?].
Navigation was very calm and better.

May 27th 1935 (Monday)
As usual, the weather was clear and a
wave was calm and there were ripples
but on the surface of the sea, it was a
glassy sea.
This ship went forward to the south
east.
The sun approached us a little bit and I
felt that heat increased.
A Chinese lady sat my next seat when at
lunchtime today.
The ship's lunch changes Western-style
food to Japanese one from day to day
but I felt that Western-style food isn't
good taste somehow.
Tonight, our ship came near to the Suez Canal.

The movie put on the screen tonight at 8.30pm.
I went to bed at 10pm.

May 28th 1935 (Tuesday)
The weather was very quiet this morning, too.
I became that I felt very hot.
I took a nap from 1pm to 3pm.
After dinner, I wrote Tokeien, Komaki-Kakinn [*both were
the Japanese hatcheries*], Inagaki-Nojyo [*his hatchery*],
Kaneichi Suzuki and Shunji the letters.
The sea was quite calm.
I chatted with the people in the hall and I went to bed at
about 10pm.

May 29th 1935 (Wednesday)
The good weather kept on every day and it was calm
voyage.
But I was bored very much with monotonous voyage.
Sleeping was my just work.

May 30th 1935 (Thursday)
This morning at 2am, the ship entered Port Said.
After breakfast, I went to in the city and I did my
shopping.
The ship sailed from
Port Said at noon two
hours behind of
schedule.

At last, the ship
entered the canal and
our ship passed the
Yasukuni Maru [a sister ship].
I heard that our ship would enter the Suez Port at this
midnight.

From today, my cabin became sixth berth room.
It became very cool from about 11pm.
There was a lot of marine traffic in this sea area.
It had to take time to run.
I went to bed at about midnight.

May 31st 1935 (Friday)
It was intense heat, I was in the Red Sea.
But it was the calm wave and the calm sea and we could see well that the bare hill on both sides coast. It was very hot and hot.
I went out on the deck and my body was damp for the sea breeze.
I was discomfited by it.

June 1st 1935 (Saturday)
Today, the steamer was at the very middle of the Red Sea.
From in the morning, it was very hot and it was windless in the daytime.
They discomforted me.
Tonight, the cinema put on the screen.
I cooled off on the boat deck and I was eased and comfortable a little.
But I was very bored, as usual.

June 2nd 1935 (Sunday)
It became to be a little cool from evening, similarly yesterday.
Tonight, I lost at cards and I treated an opponent to two bottles of lemonade.

June 3rd 1935 (Monday)
As usual, the weather was good and very hot but the

ship didn't pitch and roll.

In the afternoon, I tried to take a nap in the cabin but I couldn't sleep for heat.

I had a chat with passengers in the hall until about 11pm.

Tonight, I slept under the ceiling fan in the hall.

June 4th 1935 (Tuesday)

I got up at about 5am, because of I had slept in the hall last night.

I washed my face and I took a short rest.

It seemed that it was hot today, too.

I heard that the ship would pass out the Red Sea in the morning today.

It was hot and hot and I tried to sleep under the ceiling fan in the hall but I couldn't sleep, so I slept on the deck.

June 5th 1935 (Wednesday)

From this morning, the ship began to pitch and roll in earnest.

I had no appetite and I felt that I had fever a little because of I had slept on the deck last night.

Spray of wave entered to the cabin through the window and my bed and pillow got wet with seawater.

After all, here was the Indian Ocean and I could eat nothing. I would lose weight gradually.

June 6th 1935 (Thursday)

It was a big wave and the ship pitched and rolled very much.

I was not a semi-invalid, I was a true invalid.

I didn't have breakfast and I had been on my bed, after that I took a bath.

I tried to eat lunch but my throat didn't let any food pass.

At about 4pm, I was refreshed with a bottle of lemonade.

In the afternoon, weather was mainly cloudy and the sea was rough yet.

It was very hot but I could sleep well and as before I had no appetite at all.

My urine's colour was bright red.

June 7th 1935 (Friday)

Weather was mainly cloudy but today's wave was calmer than yesterday one and I was easy.

I became fed up with the long sea trip and I had to be patient for about twenty days.

I was waiting only my homeland.

June 8th 1935 (Saturday)

From this morning, the sea was very calm.

I had a slight headache for the past few days but I felt not so bad.

It was distant over 620 miles away from here to Colombo. I heard that the ship would arrive there at about noon on 10th.

From evening, it became a big wave on the sea and I closed my cabin's window. It was very hot in my room.

June 9th 1935 (Sunday)

I felt unusually that it was very cool today.

I was fed up by prolonged my headache.

I didn't take breakfast and I took a bath at 8am.

The menu on dinner was Sukiyaki *[traditional Japanese meat dish]* but I didn't feel well and it wasn't delicious.

I stopped to go to the cinema and I went to bed early.

June 10th 1935 (Monday)
The weather was mainly cloudy.
At noon, the ship arrived in a port in Colombo.
After lunch, I went for a walk in the city.
It was rainy weather and I returned my ship by the launch that departure time was 3.30pm.
After that, I had rest a little.
I had drunk coffee in the evening therefore I couldn't sleep.
It was very hot and hot and I was embarrassed by it.

June 11th 1935 (Tuesday)
I hadn't been able to sleep well last night so I couldn't get up early and I hadn't breakfast this morning.
At a later time, I took a bath and I went to a barber's.
After lunch, I took a little rest.
Last night, the ship pitched and rolled considerably but today, it was very cool and I was comfortable.
I could see the good moon through the window.
I went to bed at about 1am.

June 12th 1935 (Wednesday)
As usual, I got up late and I hadn't breakfast this morning.
I got up once for taking a bath and I slept in the cabin the whole day.
After dinner, I cooled myself on the deck and I felt that it got cooler.

June 13th 1935 (Thursday)

I couldn't sleep last night until about 1am for both causes, afternoon nap and it was very hot. I was discomforted by it.

In the morning, I got up at 9am and I took a bath but I didn't have breakfast.

The weather was very fine and the sea was calm. The ship didn't have pitching and rolling.

It seemed that our ship got into the Strait of Malacca.

In the afternoon, I could see a lush island to starboard.

After dinner, I played cards and I lost it tonight, too.

I was treated to a Chinese beer and I went to bed at midnight.

June 14th 1935 (Friday)

The weather was good, I didn't take breakfast and after bathing, I had a little rest.

A wave was a little high and the wave motion baptised my bed.

After lunch, I took a nap and after dinner, I washed my face.

I foretasted that I couldn't sleep well.

A Chinese girl was very pleasant and delightful.

In the morning, I took a photograph of her on the deck.

I couldn't sleep until at about 3am and I was uncomfortable by sleeplessness.

June 15th 1935 (Saturday)

I didn't have breakfast.

The ship entered in Singapore at about 4pm.

After dinner, I went for a walk in the city.

Although here was a land of everlasting summer, it was cool tonight but sometimes I sweated.

I went to Yoshino Shoten, Shinkiraku [shops/Restaurant], and Lion-Restaurant.

I got back to my ship at 11pm and I had a chat with my companions.

I could see the beautiful moon through the palm trees and I felt keenly emotions of the south seas.

June 16th 1935 (Sunday)
Last night, I could sleep well by reason of it was calm for the ship was at anchor, it was cool and I got tired.

After a long time, I had breakfast this morning.

At noon, the ship left Singapore for Hong Kong.

The sea was calm but weather was hot.

I played cards tonight and I won one game.

June 17th 1935 (Monday)
Last night, it was occasional rain and I hadn't breakfast this morning.

I was bored with my commonplace daily life at sea.

I was really uncomfortable by heat. It was very hot.

I had gone to bed at about midnight but I couldn't get to sleep because of the heat.

I broke out in sweat.

I could see the good moon through the porthole.

June 18th 1935 (Tuesday)
This morning, I could sleep well as I hadn't been able to sleep well.

I didn't take breakfast either, I washed last night's sweat away with bathing.

The ship covered 359 miles in from yesterday noon to this noon, I heard.

I felt that a day was very long.
I went to bed at midnight but I didn't fall asleep because of heat.

June 19th 1935 (Wednesday)
Every day, it was cool in the morning so I got a sleep until 8am.
I hadn't breakfast this morning, too.
It was calm navigation.
According to the schedule, the ship would enter port in Hong Kong at about 3pm.on tomorrow.
After dinner, I cooled myself on the boat deck a little while.
Later, I chatted to the cabin boy.

June 20th 1935 (Thursday)
It was a calm voyage but weather was very hot and humid.
At 5pm, the ship came alongside the pier.
After dinner, I took a stroll with Sugimoto and other three people.
We crossed over on the opposite bank by a ferryboat.
I returned to the ship at 10pm and I took a rest.
Tonight at midnight, the ship would set sail for Shanghai, I heard.

June 21st 1935 (Friday)
It was comfortable voyage.
I took breakfast and a bath.
I talked and chatted with companions in the cabin.
After dinner, I played cards and it finished at 10.40pm.
I went to bed at about 11pm.
It was a really calm sea trip.

June 22nd 1935 (Saturday)
The weather was mainly cloudy but from afternoon it was fine.
The sea was calm and the wind was favourable therefore I was felt as cool as could be on my bed.
I had been exhausted for the voyage day after day.
I got well feel and I had good feeling but I didn't want to go out into the deck so I stayed at my cabin every day.
From few days ago, I got to take breakfast because of my physical condition got well again.
I could return to my fondly remembered Japan after a few days.
I couldn't stop to smile by the indescribable mind of memories of home.
After afternoon tea, at 3pm, I went up to the deck but it was very hot as usual there.
Soon, I returned my cabin.
After dinner, I played cards until 11pm.

June 23rd 1935 (Sunday)
The expected time of arrival in Shanghai was at 3pm this afternoon but the ship was held up in a fog from about 8am until about 4pm.
For that reason, the ship would arrive there at about 3am tomorrow morning, I heard.
The waiting time was very long and we had to wait too long for restarting.
This trouble and situation confounded everyone.
The weather got better gradually and we were nearing Shanghai.

June 24th 1935 (Monday)
This morning, the weather was good and before breakfast, the ship entered Shanghai port.
After breakfast, I went to see the sights in the city and Byo-Gyo-Chin
On the way, as I looked at a battle site,[21] I could not repress my tears.
At noon, I got back to the ship and after lunch, I exchanged English currency into Japanese one.
I felt heat a little during sightseeing in the city but today's voyage was very good for it was cool and comfortable without pitching and rolling.
This conditions was first experience for me since sailing.
I asked a cabin boy to send a telegraph for me to tonight.
Supper tonight, was late.

June 25th 1935 (Tuesday)
This morning, I slept until at 9am and I didn't have breakfast but I took a bath.
After lunch, I took a nap.
It was calm sea as a glassy one.
From about 4pm, I arranged my things.
It became one day more from now to Japan.

June 26th 1935 (Wednesday)
This morning, the weather is fine.
I didn't take breakfast for I got up late.
At about 8am, I took a bath and I went out into the deck.
At about 10am, the ship passed through the Kanmon Strait and I could look at Japanese houses and Japanese boats on either bank.

---

[21] Japanese/Chinese "Battle for Shanghai" – January 28th – March 3rd 1932. (Only three years previously.)

All things were my happy and sweet memories.

It was calm voyage.

We had a drink for our farewell tonight.

I went bed at midnight, but I couldn't get to sleep so I was restless.

June 27th 1935 (Thursday)

I got up at 4am and I was very busy by preparations for to leave the ship.

At 6am, I finished customs inspection and procedures.

At 8am, I left the ship.[22]

I went straight to Nagoya[23] at the 10.44 train.

Mr Inagaki *[Employer]*, Mr Yamaguchi *[the Chairman of board of directors of the Japanese Chicken Sexing Association]*, Mr Maeno *[a relative]*, my Mother *[Kimi]*, Tadaichi *[Brother]* and Mr Kojima *[Brother-in-Law]* came out and meet me.[24]

---

[22] According to YYK Line records the Hakusan Maru did not call at Nagoya Port on return legs. So he probably disembarked at Osaka or Kobe to get a train to Nagoya and then home.

[23] Nagoya was about 20km from his home in Komaki.

[24] The order of people listed is typically how Japanese would prioritise the importance of people in their lives. Work superiors and colleagues were and are often seen as closer than family.

So, what became of Koichi Andoh?

It is not clear what happened to Koichi immediately on his return to Japan. It is likely that he continued to work in the chicken industry in Nagoya until he was sent his 'red paper' conscripting him into the Japanese Army in August 1941 (four months before Pearl Harbour). From what records are available it seems he was conscripted into the Eastern 88th Unit, in Sagamihara, Japan (a Homeland or Domestic Unit probably offering basic training). He was later transferred to the 3rd Telegraph Regiment. The records and correspondence he sent home show he was sent to Korea and Manchuria until December 1942 when he was posted to Rabaul on New Britain, New Guinea. The 3rd Telegraph Regiment was by then part of the newly formed 18th Army sent to defend the South Pacific against the allies. It is believed he was a radio operator as well as being an infantryman.

It is hard to imagine what a young and obviously sensitive Japanese man, who had breached the cultural divide of East and West, would have thought about his country being at war with the British just a few years after his time England.

According to Australian government estimates, backed by Japanese demobilization documentation, by the end of the war in the Pacific, around 150,000 Japanese troops had served on mainland New Guinea; of these 120,000 died and 30,000 eventually surrendered. A further 2,400 later died of injuries or disease. Koichi's wartime movements were recorded as being along the north coast of New Guinea including Aitabe, Madang, Wewak. A comrade, who made it home after the war, told Koichi's family that Koichi had died of shrapnel injuries to the chest at Karawop near Wewak on 5th October 1944.

In Britain we still hear the stories from our parents and grandparents of the terrible cruelty inflicted on POWs by the Japanese army. But as was graphically depicted in the acclaimed film *Letters from Iwo Jima*, (directed by Clint Eastwood, 2006), some elements of the Japanese military were equally cruel to their own conscripts. As a result thousands of Japanese who might have surrendered fought on to the end, as for them the alternative was death anyway, at the hands of their fanatical officers. We know Koichi was a conscript, and when we read his emotional comments in the diary, of 24th June 1935, about visiting the former battlefield in Shanghai, we might justly speculate that he would have been a reluctant combatant and less likely to be caught up in the cultural honour-code of imperial/national duty, 'death or shame'. Personally, I prefer to believe he was just another human victim of war, a simple man passionate about his occupation, who, like millions of others on all sides, was taken away from his settled world and obliged to fight for his own survival. He had his life cut short and in his beloved but devastated homeland Koichi left behind his pregnant widow and the two-year-old Takayoshi.

For Mr Takayoshi Andoh and his family this book is dedicated to:

'Peace, friendship and understanding in the World'

Takayoshi Andoh
near where his father worked in Hebden Bridge.

Appendix 1
Koichi's Colleagues:

Mr Yamaguchi *[the Chairman of board of directors of the Japanese Chicken Sexing Association]*. This man seems to be a very important man in the industry. References appear in the 1930s poultry press, to him having been a pioneer in taking the sexing techniques to the USA and lecturing.

Mr Nishitani (Mitsuo) – The 'relationship' evidence in the diary suggests that Mr Nishitani worked as some sort of representative for the association, based in Hebden Bridge, but travelling around making arrangements for paying wages, placing the Japanese sexers with hatcheries, etc. The role seems to be a supervisory one. But he does socialise with the sexers. He lived in Hebden Bridge with Slater Greenwood, in Palace House Road.

Mr Ikuta, based in Portman Sq., London. He seemed to have had overall agent responsibility for the placing of Japanese sexers in Britain.

Mr. Kennosuke Ishima lived in London –
responsibilities unknown

Koichi Andoh on far right

Japanese Chicken Sexers:
Mr Hattori – c/o Mr H W Dickie, 141 Keighley Rd.,
Cowling, Yorks.
Mr Itoh – c/o Mr Spinks, Prospect Farm, Easingwold,
York.
Mr Sugano – c/o Mr G Gill, Manor Farm, Broadway,
Weymouth.
Mr Kumei - c/o Mr Black, The Bays, Lydd, Kent.
Mr Kuno – c/o Mr W D Evans, Kibworth Hatchery,
Leicestershire.
        Also c/o Mr G Hamer, Moss Hill Farm,
Bradshaw, Bolton, Lancs.
Mr Takabatake – c/o Mr Cranfield, School House,
Bleatsoe, Bedfordshire.
        Also c/o Mr W D Evans, Kibworth
Hatchery, Leicestershire.

124

Mr Terazawa –Watson's & Thornber's Hatcheries, Hebden Bridge - Lodgings – Watson's.

Mr Katsuzo (Moribe) – Watson's & Thornber's Hatcheries, Hebden Bridge - Lodgings – Watson's.

Mr Ise

Mr Shinohara

Mr Kamio

Koichi's Colleagues in Japan

Mr Matsunaga – Head of the agricultural association.

Mr Kato – Association.

Mr Ochiai – Training school farm.

Mr Inagaki – Koichi's Employer

Mr Inagaki

Family

Tadaichi – Brother,

Chiyoko – Sister

Shunji – Brother

Kiichi Kojima – Brother in law

Saburo Kojima – Younger brother of Kiichi

Mr Yamaishi Inagaki – Relative [not related to Koichi's employer].
Kumiko – Cousin
Mr Ikeda – Relative
Yasucchi – Cousin
Mr Maeno – Relative
Kumei – Relative
Higashitanaka – Relative
Komatsuji – Relative

Others Mentioned
Mr Niwa – Village Headman/Elder
Mr Kaneichi Suzuki – Friend
Mr Nakane – Neighbour
Mr Okawa
Mr Ise
Mr Tanaguchi
Mr Shiohara
Mr Ishioka
Sueo Osada – old school friend
Mr Sugimoto

Appendix 2

Films they saw at the Hebden Picture House in 1935

Dates from the Diary:

Jan 12th – 'Freedom of the Seas' – A Comedy with Clifford Mollison & Wendie Barrie.

Jan 26th – 'Say it with flowers' – A Musical

Feb 12th – 'One is Guilty' – Mystery Romance with Ralph Bellamy & Shirley Grey
Also 'Born to be Bad' with Loretta Young & Cary Grant.

Mar 30th – 'Singeree' – About an Australian Outlaw with Irene Dunn & Richard Dix.

Apr 6th – 'The Last Stallion' – A Comedy with George Arliss.

Apr 9th – 'The Lost Jungle' – A Melodrama about Lion Tamer going Hand to Hand with Wild Animals.

Apr 13th – 'Nell Gwyn' – With Anna Neagle, Cedric Hardwicke.

Apr 19th – 'White Ensign' – About Navy life. 'A sterling yarn' with Molly Lamont & Ivan Sampson. *[But they couldn't get in – tickets all sold.]*

Apr 27th – 'Blossom Time' – Musical with Richard Tauber & Jane Baxter.

Appendix 3

Documentation

The original Diary cover

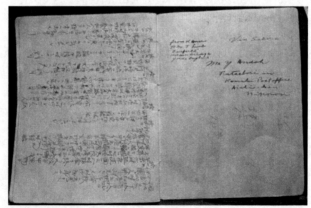

First page of diary, showing Lumb's and Koichi's address

With Compliments from

F. & T. LUMB

Winners S P N A W N E L

Breeders of Competition Winners
and Pedigree Utility Poultry. Eggs
for Hatching and Day-old Chicks
a Speciality. Stock Birds and
Breeding Pens.

1935

Fairfield, HEBDEN BRIDGE, Yorks.

Telephone 193.　　　　　　　　　　　Telegrams : "Lumb, Fairfield, Hebden Bridge."

F. & T. LUMB
BREEDERS OF COMPETITION WINNING POULTRY

Postal Address: FAIRFIELD, HEBDEN BRIDGE, Yorks.
Proprietor—T. LUMB.

Dear Sir or Madam,

We have great pleasure in forwarding to you our Catalogue for 1935. May we take this opportunity of offering to all our patrons and new customers, our best wishes for the coming year? We accept new clients with the greatest of pleasure, and our services are always at your command. Having been actual poultry farmers for 25 years, and a life-time's experience (54 years) in poultry and farming, you may rest assured that every item in this Catalogue results from practical experience.

We have an up-to-date hatchery, giving a total Egg capacity of 230,000 eggs, and all run by electricity. The Chicks hatched in these machines are larger than Chicks hatched with ordinary machines.

Our stock has roomy grass runs. The farm is 1,000 feet above sea level, very bleak and cold, thus ensuring the hardiest stock and more excellent results. In feeding we aim at healthy, vigorous stock, giving steady production of eggs that will hatch sturdy, vigorous Chicks. Our stock is fed and managed as breeding stock all the year round, so as to produce sturdy Chicks during the Spring, and must say that our stock is better to-day than ever before, because our breeders are all selected birds for size of body, size of egg and stamina. Just the type for egg production.

Every order for Eggs, Chicks or Stock Birds will receive special attention and will be despatched promptly. No order too small and Day-old Chicks can be supplied in One Dozen to 5,000 in one delivery.

A short notice is required for 5,000 Chicks in one delivery. The Day-old Chicks we supply are most wonderful in size and quality. They are real beauties; just try them, they will pay you well and are good to rear.

Your stock depends mainly on improved stock. Bear in mind always that increased Egg production is transmitted through the influence of the Male bird. We offer no Cockerels unless they are sons of a Dam, who in her pullet year was herself a prolific layer. Whether sittings of Eggs, Stock Cockerels, Chicks or Breeding Pens are required, consult us, we have the best. Progress with your poultry during the coming year will mainly depend upon improved stock. To assist you we have carefully mated all pens which are sure to produce abundance of Eggs. When orders are booked from Extra Special Pens we guarantee every Egg or Chick to come from the Special Pen as ordered. There are a large number of Pens equally as good and better, which are not catalogued. Any Pen or Pens may be altered if by any season we desire.

Page one

Lumb's Hatchery Brochure

129

FOR READERS' INFORMATION

Much disappointment can be avoided if clients will place their orders as much ahead as possible. If a special date is appointed you have our assurance that same will be duly delivered, but when orders are casually received, they can only be executed in rotation.

To anyone wishing to visit our Farm, we shall be only too pleased to show anyone round.

We are only two minutes' walk from Hebden Bridge Station. If coming by Tram, 'Bus or Car, turn off the main road at the Station Road, and from there Brick Buildings and Brooder Houses can be seen, and it is only 5 minutes' walk.

TERMS OF SALE

CHICKS, Live Delivery in Free Boxes, Carriage Paid, Passenger Train. Any dying in transit will be replaced or credited, provided they are returned at once, Carriage Paid. WE CANNOT ACCEPT RESPONSIBILITY FOR LOSS IN REARING OR LOSS IN PROFIT CAUSED THEREBY, as all Stock is BLOOD-TESTED each year before the breeding season commences, which makes loss beyond our control.

Orders for Delivery on a specified date will be accepted, providing cash is sent or deposited with any Poultry Paper, 7 clear days before the date due for Chicks to be despatched.

Special Chicks, 3/- per dozen extra than the advertised prices.

Ordinary Pens are at prices advertised in Poultry Papers.

SITTINGS OF EGGS.—Hatching Eggs from Pens or Flocks are of the very best and we guarantee hatchability. Special Egg Boxes will be used to insure safe delivery, but they must be returned, or 6d. in stamps. When placing orders always give the nearest Station in BLOCK LETTERS. Cash must accompany order or, deposit with any Poultry Paper.

Any sale effected under quotation, or descibed in invoice, is subject to the following:—Section XIV. (Sub-Section 1 and 2) of the Sale of Goods Act, 1893, or at Common Law, are expressly excluded from the said sale.

BANKERS:—THE DISTRICT BANK LIMITED.

Page two

LAYING TESTS RESULTS

1925—Lancashire International Laying Test; 5 R.I. Reds winning 1st place and Silver Cup and First Class Pen Certificate, with 1,048 eggs : 1.077 points—value £8 8s. 8½d.—for a period of 48 weeks. The 12 months' record being 1,145 eggs, which we claim to be one of the finest records for R.I. Reds over all England Laying Tests during 1925.

1926—Lancashire International Laying Test : Single Bird Test—White Wyandotte laid 271 eggs in 48 weeks. Awarded 1st Class Certificate.

1926—Midland Laying Test : 4 R.I. Reds awarded Silver Medal for 2nd place, 2/2¾ behind the Cup Winners; 4 White Leghorns awarded Diploma.

1927—Serial Laying Test : 4 White Leghorns awarded Silver Medal for 2nd place.

1927—Yorkshire Laying Test : R.I. Reds awarded 3 Second-Class Certificates; White Leghorns, 1 Second-Class Certificate, also copper numbered Ring; admission of its record into the Official Register of the National Poultry Council.

1928—Serial Laying Test, Skegness, Lincolnshire; 5 White Leghorns winning Silver Cup outright and £25 Cash Prize over all light breeds.

1928—Yorkshire Laying Test at Otley, Yorkshire : Hebden Bridge Poultry Society had one Pen of White Wyandottes in the Heavy Section and one Pen of White Leghorns in the Light Team Section, and am very pleased to say that our two teams won the Silver Cup and £3 3s. 0d. in cash in each section. Also 14 Bronze Medals of which we had 2 White Wyandottes and 1 White Leghorn in these Pens. This made us winners of 3 Bronze Medals and 27/- Cash Prize.

1929—Serial Laying Test, Skegness : 4 White Leghorns winning Silver Cup and Cash Prize over all Light Breeds at the Test.

1929—Yorkshire Laying Test : Hebden Bridge Poultry Society's Team of which some of the members had one bird each, and our White Leghorn won the Gold Medal by being the best bird in the Team.

1933—Mirfield Laying Test : Our Pen of White Leghorns gained 2nd place and Silver Medal, and R.I. Red Pullet in Single Bird Section also won Silver Medal for 2nd place.

1934—Yorkshire Laying Test : 1st and 2nd Class Certificates.

Page three

Lumb's Hatchery Brochure, page 3

Terms of Business

(1) All offers, sales, or agreements for sale are subject to the following :—
All terms, conditions and warranties, either expressed or implied by Section 14 (Sub-section 1 and 2) of the Sale of Goods Act, 1893, or at Common Law are expressly excluded from any sale effected under the foregoing quotation or described in Invoice or any other document forming the basis of any contract between the vendor and the purchaser. No liability will be accepted under any circumstances whether arising consequentially or otherwise.
These conditions are the terms upon which all sales are made by us unless a specially written contract is signed.

(2) Payment.
Cash with order or on receipt of invoice unless otherwise arranged. We reserve the right to re-sell any chicks not paid for 3 days before delivery.

(3) Quotations.
All quotations carriage paid, except where otherwise stated, and subject to being unsold on receipt of order.

(4) Delivery.
Live delivery is guaranteed.
(a) *Day-old Chicks.* A credit will be made for any chicks dying on rail, provided both legs are returned to us immediately.
(b) *Growing and adult stock.* Any birds dying on rail will be replaced or cash refunded at our option if returned immediately.

(5) Whilst every precaution is taken, no liability can be accepted for failing to deliver, or to deliver to time, due to unfertility of eggs, seasonal conditions, fire, disease, mechanical breakdown, war conditions, or other occurrence over which we have no control.
All livestock ordered unseen must be inspected by the purchaser immediately on delivery and if not as ordered may be returned, but if the buyer does not inform the vendor within twelve hours of delivery that he is returning the livestock he shall be deemed to have accepted delivery in performance of the contract, and the seller accepts no liability for any loss howsoever arising.

(6) Sex or Sex-Linked Pullets.
We guarantee not less than 95 pullets in 100.

47	,,	50.
23	,,	25.
11	,,	12.

Should it be found that there are more cockerels than the numbers referred to above, and provided we are notified when chicks are between the ages of 10 and 14 weeks, we will refund the purchase price of all cockerels in excess of our guarantee. We reserve the right to request the return of cockerels for inspection.

(7) We reserve the right to cancel any order, and to discontinue supplying any customer if we see fit.

Hatchery's Terms of Sale

In search of those sexy chicks his father knew...

Robert Sutcliffe

A JAPANESE man has made an emotional 5,000-mile trip to Hebden Bridge to retrace his father's steps after discovering diaries detailing his time there in the 1930s... as an expert chicken sexer.

Takayoshi Andoh, 62, a retired gas worker, had only heard about his father's visit from his grandparents, but a few years ago he found the diaries in a trunk hidden away in an old storeroom.

Since then he has planned to visit the town where his father Koichi arrived with Japanese colleagues at the age of 25 in January 1935, after a 42-day voyage.

The exchange visit was organised by the Japanese Society for Determining the Sex of Chickens.

From snatches of the diaries which Mr Andoh jnr has translated into English it seems his father enjoyed his six-month stay, though his inability to speak the language fluently made things difficult.

He stayed with the Lumb family of Fairfield, who ran a hatchery, and took his work extremely seriously, sexing 1,800 chickens in a day, with a success rate of 95 per cent. He was later killed in New Guinea during the Second World War, when he was about 34 and Takayoshi only a tot.

Although Mr Andoh was unable to meet any of the Lumb family, he did meet Lloyd Greenwood, 76, who is related by marriage to the Lumbs and was able to fill him in on much of the background to his father's visit.

"I remember them coming, though I was only a boy at the time," said Mr Greenwood. "It was rather strange having foreigners about in those days.

"I think they came over because they were more adept at sexing chickens than we were. At that time Hebden Bridge and Mytholmroyd were famous for hatching chickens, and we used to send millions of day-old chicks all over the country by rail."

Mr Andoh said yesterday: "It's been a success. I had wanted to meet the Lumb children or grandchildren, but this meeting was much more than I had ever hoped for.

"I have seen the original site where the hatchery where he worked is, and found out all sorts of other interesting information. My mother, Kimi, will be pleased to hear all about it."

Yorkshire Post,
18 September
2001

Takayoshi Andoh: 5,000-mile trip to scene of his father's great adventure.

Japanese visitor to Hebden Bridge

in the steps of an illustrious ancestor

Following in father's footsteps

A JAPANESE man made an emotional visit to Hebden Bridge to find out more about the father he cannot remember.

Mr Takayoshi Andoh was only two years old when his father Koichi died. But while clearing out a warehouse near his home he found a diary belonging to his father, which mentioned the time he spent in Hebden Bridge in the 1930s.

He had come to the area on a six-month exchange programme to work at the former F&T Lumb Hatchery at Fairfield. It was his job to distinguish the sex of one-day-old chicks.

Mr Andoh speaks little English and Mr Stephen Curry, who owns Angeldale Guest House, Hebden Bridge, where Mr Andoh is staying, said he had come to Britain for an English course.

"He had the motivation to come to Hebden Bridge and find out more about his father's time here," he said.

First he went to Hebden Bridge Tourist Information Centre which put him in touch with local historian Mr Lloyd Greenwood.

It turned out that Mr Greenwood was related by marriage to the family Mr Andoh's father stayed with while in Hebden Bridge.

Although Mr Greenwood does not remember Mr Andoh's father he remembers other Japanese workers and showed him where the hatchery used to be. Mr Andoh has also been put in contact with one of the former factory owner's sons, Mr Ernest Lumb, who lives in Harrogate. He has been unable to visit him but intends to write.

Mr Andoh said people had offered to try to find out information about his father. "I now feel satisfied and thank everybody so much for being so kind," he said.

Takayoshi Ando searching for information in Hebden Bridge

Halifax Evening Courier, 19 September 2001

Son's nostalgic journey to retrace his father's steps

By Francesca Turner

DIARIES found in an old trunk have prompted a Japanese man to fly 5,000 miles to Hebden Bridge to retrace time his father spent here in 1935 - as an expert chick sexer.

Takayoshi Andoh, a 61-year-old retired gas worker from Komaki City, arrived at the town's tourist information centre last Saturday hoping to discover some of the people and places described in his father's old letters and journals.

He had previously written to the last known address of the Hebden Bridge family his father had stayed with, but the letter returned unopened.

Four years before the outbreak of war, Koichi Andoh arrived in Britain with three Japanese colleagues after a 42-day voyage. The men were expert chicken sexers, and the exchange had been organised by the Japanese Society for Determining the Sex of One-Day-Old Poultry.

At the time, Hebden Bridge and Mytholmroyd were famous for their hatcheries and millions of day-old chicks were sent all over the country by rail. But sexing chicks is surprisingly difficult, and the Japanese were world-renowned for their excellence at it.

From the diaries - which Takayoshi has translated into English - it appears that his father much enjoyed his six month stay with the Lumb family of Fairfield, who ran a major poultry business in Hebden Bridge.

He worked hard and often sexed 1,800 chicks a day with a success rate of 95 per cent. Koichi was later killed in New Guinea during the Second World War when Takayoshi was only a tot.

Hearing his story, staff at the tourist information centre alerted local historian Lloyd Greenwood who is related by marriage to the Lumbs and remembered his own father discussing the town's oriental visitors.

During his brief stay, Lloyd escorted Takayoshi round many places of personal interest in Hebden Bridge. "He was very polite and bowed a lot," said Lloyd. "And I couldn't help thinking how strange it was that I went to war with his country and that his father had died fighting."

Before returning to Japan, Takayoshi said this meeting had given him "much more than I had ever hoped for."

Stephen Curry, proprietor of the Angeldale Guest House in Hebden Bridge where Takayoshi stayed, said: "Many things may have changed in the 66 years since his father was here, but Mr Andoh left feeling the people of Hebden Bridge were just as kind and helpful to him as they were to his father all those years ago."

• An inscribed marble urn from "Mitsu," one of Koichi's Japanese colleagues, can still be seen on a grave at Heptonstall Slack expressing respect and affection for members of the family buried there who gave him lodgings during his stay.

Retracing his father'd footsteps: Takayoshi Andoh

Hebden Bridge Times, 21 September 2001

133

Appendix 4

Photo Gallery

The Journey

*From top, Koichi unknown venue; 'Arabia'; Koichi &
colleagues, unknown venue*

From top, Koichi, fellow passengers & crew; Koichi and others; Koichi with colleagues and fellow passengers.

Above: party taking tea on the Hakusan-Maru.
Below: party time on the Hakusan-Maru.

Above: Koichi on deck and colleagues homeward bound.

Japan docking.

Mildred Butterworth & colleague packing one-day-old chicks at Finney Brothers' Hatchery

L-R: Thomas Lumb, William (Willy) Watson and Ernest Wood

Koichi and Moribe

Renée Wilcock and Donald Sutcliffe

Group at Willy Watson's house, 'Stoneleigh'

The Watson twins, Phyllis (L) & Doris, with baby Stephen Barker

Thomas Lumb (L) & Herbert Henry Sutcliffe; Minnie Sutcliffe (L) & Amy Lumb behind.

Slater Greenwood's grave with Mitsuo's urn
(Slack Top Cemetery)

Letter to Mr Lumb from Koichi,
written on ship's notepaper, perhaps with assistance.

Family-run hatchery, Japan

Hatchery owner's children

143

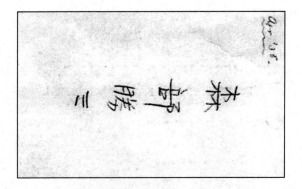

KATSUZO MORIBE,
DISCRIMINATING EXPERT OF CHICKS.

C/O SUZUKI POULTRY FARM,
4 NAOKI—CHO,
MINAMI—KU,
NAGOYA, JAPAN.

Moribe's Business Card

Above and right: Koichi Andoh at home

Mrs Kimi Andoh (in white) working at home making silkworm trays.

The family together with Koichi's parents (Yosokichi & Kinu) and Tayakoshi as a small child. Mr Andoh is wearing a Fundoshi. This may be the last photo before he was killed.

Mrs Andoh (front right) with other war widows at a shrine.

Lightning Source UK Ltd.
Milton Keynes UK
UKOW040434010812

196835UK00002B/6/P